CREATING YOUR GRIEF PLAN:

The Power of Understanding and Befriending the Six Universal Needs of Mourning

ALAN D. WOLFELT, PH.D.

ALSO BY ALAN WOLFELT

Understanding Your Grief:
Ten Essential Touchstones for Finding Hope and Healing Your Grief

Companioning the Bereaved:
A Soulful Guide for Caregivers

Healing Your Grieving Heart:
100 Practical Ideas

Grief One Day at a Time:
365 Meditations to Help You Heal After Loss

You're Not Crazy – You're Grieving:
6 Steps for Surviving Loss

Stay for the Cup of Coffee:
How to Support Others in Grief

CREATING YOUR GRIEF PLAN:

The Power of Understanding and Befriending the Six Universal Needs of Mourning

ALAN D. WOLFELT, PH.D.

Companion
PRESS

Fort Collins, Colorado
An imprint of the Center for Loss and Life Transition

Companion
PRESS

Companion Press is dedicated to the education and support of both the bereaved and bereavement caregivers. We believe that those who companion the bereaved by walking with them as they journey in grief have a wondrous opportunity: to help others embrace and grow through grief—and to lead fuller, more deeply-lived lives themselves because of this important ministry.

For a complete catalog and ordering information, write or call:
Companion Press
The Center for Loss and Life Transition
3735 Broken Bow Road
Fort Collins, CO 80526
(970) 226-6050
www.centerforloss.com

Companion Press is an imprint of the
Center for Loss and Life Transition
3735 Broken Bow Road
Fort Collins, Colorado 80526

Printed in the United States of America

30 29 28 27 26 25 5 4 3 2 1

ISBN: 978-1-61722-341-9

IN MEMORY

This book is dedicated to my brother,
Gary Wolfelt, who died suddenly and unexpectedly
while I was writing this book.

He was a good man who touched many lives.

TABLE OF CONTENTS

WELCOME

"All sorrows can be borne if we put them in a story or tell a story about them."

– Isak Dinesen

The death of someone precious to us changes our lives forever. I discovered this reality during my teenage years when several of my family members and friends died. I was shocked and disappointed that no one talked about the deaths. It was as if the deaths never happened, yet inside me I was experiencing deep pain and many new and confusing thoughts and feelings. What's more, **no one helped me make a plan for what I was to do with my overwhelming grief.**

Even as a child, I could see that our culture doesn't do grief well. In fact, it was then that I decided that when I grew up, I would try to be a force for change and an advocate for grieving people. I wrote my mission statement for what would eventually become my Center for Loss & Life Transition at age 16. I knew then I would make it my life's work to evolve our culture's understanding of grief and how to support one another after a loss.

Now, I've been a grief counselor for over 40 years and have developed a model anchored in "companioning" my fellow human beings, not "treating" them. As I've had the honor of companioning thousands of grievers, I have come to understand the importance of taking action to help integrate loss into one's life. I call this your GRIEF PLAN.

This book, directed from my heart to your heart, is an invitation to make a plan for what to do with your raw grief. In large part, this book is about helping you engage in six universal needs of mourning. I sincerely hope it can be a companion to you as you ride the waves of grief during this naturally challenging time of your life.

This book is not in any way intended to help you "let go," "put your grief behind you," or "experience closure." Instead, I will help you make a GRIEF PLAN anchored in self-compassion and personal grace.

We meet here because your heart is broken. You need and deserve support as you allow yourself to mourn. You also need and deserve a compassionate GRIEF PLAN to help you discover continued meaning and purpose in your life, your living, and your loving!

Distinguishing Grief from Mourning

That formal-sounding word bereavement means "to be torn apart" and to have some "unique needs." I believe we come into the world organically equipped to mourn our life losses. We come to **grief** when losses touch our lives and then we are faced with the need to allow ourselves to **authentically mourn**. So, a critical part of making a GRIEF PLAN is to learn to allow your grief to become mourning.

Grief is everything you think and feel on the inside. You instinctively think and feel many different things when someone you are attached to dies. This person has often brought pleasure into your life, infused safety and security, and helped form your identity. And hopefully they have added meaning and purpose to your life.

In other words, grief is what goes on inside of you related to the loss. Grief is the container – it is a single word for a big experience consisting of a multitude of thoughts and feelings.

Mourning, on the other hand, is when you take your inner grief and express it outside of yourself in some way. Whereas grief is internal, mourning is external. Grief is feeling, thinking, turning inward, remembering, and pondering. Mourning is acting, doing, creating, and moving.

Essentially, mourning is putting your grief into motion. It is the motion that creates momentum and change. That is why it is so important to create a grief/mourning plan. Doing this allows you to commit to doing the "hard work of mourning." I often say that grief waits on welcome, not on time. Time can help, but only if you learn to befriend the six needs of mourning that I'll go on to describe in the pages ahead.

AUTHENTIC MOURNING

You will note that I use the words "authentic mourning." Authentic mourning is the outward expression of your thoughts and feelings in a completely open and honest way. It is about expressing your grief without shame. This requires being congruent, where your outer words and behaviors align with your inner thoughts and feelings. I suggest you think of grief as a wheel and mourning as the engine that turns the wheel. The wheel is absolutely necessary, but to get anywhere with it, you also need to authentically mourn.

Mourning is Instinctive

We come into this world knowing how to mourn. From the moment we take our first breaths, we respond to distress by crying. When we are distraught infants, we tip our heads back and move our arms and legs. As we grow into toddlerhood, we learn to protest when we are upset. When we are small children and teenagers we express our grief through behaviors and words.

So, we are built to mourn. And the very fact that we are capable of mourning teaches us that we are meant to gently face life losses and work to integrate them into our lives.

Our very nature, like nature itself, is intended to befriend losses rather than deny them. Each and every one of the givens of life represents some form or shape of loss. I sincerely believe that each one of us has the obligation and responsibility to attend to our life losses with passion and purpose.

However, our society often encourages prematurely moving away from grief instead of toward it. This can put you at risk for grieving in isolation or attempting to deny, suppress, or run away from your grief through various means. If we get contaminated by our emotion-phobic culture, we can lose the opportunity to embrace the grace that difficult life conditions demand.

GRACE

The proactive acceptance, love, and caring for one's fellow human beings and oneself. Grace expands your will by giving you courage you did not have before. Grace invites you to befriend your grief and mourn your life losses.

Grief, when denied or ignored, can result in what I call "carried grief." When you experience a loss but do not mourn the normal and necessary feelings of grief, you "carry" that grief forward into your future. This carried grief can result in a muting, if not extinguishing, of your **divine spark** – "that which gives depth and purpose to your living." When your divine spark is muted there is an ongoing drag on your ability to live life with meaning and purpose. In fact, when you inhibit the instinctual need to mourn, you risk being among the "living dead."

Facing your life losses is how you will discover the freedom to live until you die. It is up to you to allow for the mourning that all of life's losses require. It is up to you to learn to trust that authentic mourning is how you integrate losses and rise again to what comes next. This is how healing begins. Without a GRIEF PLAN, I find that many people stumble through grief with the faint idea that maybe one day they will wake up and time will have healed the wound.

Unfortunately, grief doesn't work that way. To heal grief, you need a plan. To make a plan, you need hope, courage, and faith.

CREATING YOUR GRIEF PLAN REQUIRES HOPE, COURAGE, AND FAITH

Hope

"How many would have failed except that hope sustained them through the darkness...until light could become dawn."

– Joan Walsh Anglund

My favorite definition of hope is that it is an expectation of a good that is yet to be. It is an inner knowing that the future holds positive things. It is the trust that no matter your current circumstances, the days to come will reveal a renewed capacity to allow joy and happiness into your life.

Without doubt, the capacity to befriend hope will lift your spirits. To befriend literally means you are making an effort to "become friends" with hope. In creating a GRIEF PLAN, you yourself can and will be the purveyor of your hope. You cultivate hope in yourself by actively engaging with and expressing your grief as well as regularly setting and affirming your intention to heal.

Befriending hope is no different than what you do when you cultivate other relationships in your life. You cultivate a relationship with hope by believing it has value, making time for it, and spending time nurturing and maintaining it by communicating with it on a regular basis. Creating a GRIEF PLAN will help you cultivate hope for your healing.

Courage

"Whatever you do, you need courage."

- Ralph Waldo Emerson

Courage is the ability to do what one believes is right, even though others may strongly or persuasively disagree. It comes from the old French word "Coeur" meaning "heart." When loss wounds your heart, the wound creates an opening for you to engage with as you muster the courage to authentically mourn.

The reality is that grief demands courage at almost every turn. It takes fortitude to rise and face the day when you know it will be filled with the pain of missing the person who died. It takes courage to let tears fall without immediately wiping them away. And it takes courage to let grief and mourning come without trying to deny them or numb yourself with distractions.

In some ways, courage is quiet and humble. It serves as the bridge between any fear you might have about allowing yourself to mourn openly and honestly. It is the still, quiet voice inside you encouraging you to befriend your grief.

Ask yourself: Do you have any fears about the prospect of being open and honest in expressing your grief? Are you someone who has never learned to be outwardly emotional? Are you afraid of losing control, whether in public or in private? Do you have certain feelings that you are ashamed of or that are difficult to talk about? Do you have family and friends who don't know how to be present to your emotions and expressions of grief?

To have some apprehension about mourning is not at all unusual. Yet, I encourage you to muster the courage to give attention to any and all fears you might have. Tackle them in tiny steps, one day at a time. Doing so as part of your GRIEF PLAN creates **divine momentum**. This is the experience of being propelled toward healing by doing what is helpful and necessary.

Faith

"The greatest act of faith some days is to simply get up and face another day."

– Amy Gatliff

Faith is a belief or trust in someone or something; even without proof. When someone in our life dies, faith and spirituality instinctively come to the forefront. I often reflect on how exploring our faith/spirituality/philosophy of life helps us "hold our sorrows." Naturally, in the face of life losses big questions arise like, "Where did they go?" "Is there a God?" "Will we meet again?" There is no spiritual bypass to the hard work of mourning.

I sincerely believe that grief sets us off on a spiritual journey because it forces us to examine our most fundamental beliefs and feelings about why we are here and what life means. To me, this means allowing yourself to engage with huge questions and the deepest, most meaningful stirrings of your heart in whatever ways you choose. Death also has a way of quickly helping us put our priorities in order – "What really matters and how do I want to live my life?"

You may well be questioning your faith or finding that your beliefs have been impacted now that you have experienced the death of someone precious to you. You may even feel angry with God or your Higher Power, feel betrayed, or have questions that don't seem to have answers.

Along the way as you create your GRIEF PLAN, I suggest you allow yourself to question your beliefs and re-define what your faith/spirituality/philosophy of life means to you. In my experience, those who do not search, do not find. Perhaps it will be helpful to remember that mystery – which is the ancient name for God – literally means something to be pondered, not explained.

As you create your GRIEF PLAN my hope is that the actions you take will help you not only get through the day, but to experience grace, see silver linings, and make use of hope, courage, and faith in ways that are meaningful to you.

UNDERSTANDING WHAT SHAPES YOUR GRIEF AND MOURNING

"This moment, this day, this relationship, this life are all exquisite, unique, and unrepeatable."

– Daphne Rose Kingma

Before you can create an action-oriented GRIEF PLAN, allow me to briefly introduce you to the things that naturally influence how your grief is experienced. Our grief journeys are never precisely the same. Be careful about comparing your experiences with that of other people. You will grieve and mourn in your own singular way.

What I want to do here is reflect on some of the unique reasons your grief is what it is – the "whys" of your particular journey. I'll invite you to make some notes about each of the influences I describe and this will help you create your GRIEF PLAN.

NON-LOVING RELATIONSHIPS AND GRIEF

While grief and love/attachment usually go hand in hand, and you will find I use the phrase "death of someone loved" throughout this book, I would be remiss if I did not also clearly state up front that not all relationships that result in grief are anchored in love. Abusive, ambivalent, and difficult relationships can be naturally challenging to openly and honestly mourn. Sometimes absent relationships are as well, because it is human nature to grieve for what might have been. After a death, people often grieve what they never had but always longed for in a relationship. Please keep this important caveat in mind as you read this book and create your GRIEF PLAN.

Your Relationship with the Person Who Died

People are unique and so are their relationships. Your relationship with the person who died was different from your relationship with anyone else. Whatever the nature and circumstances of the relationship, you are the best person to describe them. If someone asked you to describe your relationship with the person who died, what would immediately come to your mind and heart?

The Circumstances of the Death

How, why, and when the person died has a significant influence on your grief. For example, was the death sudden or anticipated? How old was the person who died? Do you feel you might have been able to prevent the death from occurring?

Describe the circumstances of the death:

The People in Your Life

Mourning serves as a signal to the people in your life that you are hurting and you need their empathy and support. Without a stabilizing support system of at least one other person (hopefully more), it becomes difficult to integrate grief into your life. You yourself are also a part of this support equation. Even when you have a solid support system in place, you must be willing and able to accept the support.

Do you have people in your life (family and friends) whom you can turn to for help and support surrounding your grief? Who are these people? Are you able to accept the support they offer?

Your Unique Personality

Whatever your unique personality may be, rest assured it will be reflected in the expression of your grief. For example, if you are quiet by nature, you may express your grief quietly. If you are outgoing, you may be more naturally expressive with your grief. Other aspects of your personality – such as your self-esteem, values, and beliefs – also impact your response to the death. In addition, any pre-existing mental health history will probably influence your grief as well.

How do you think your personality is influencing your grief and mourning?

The Unique Personality of the Person Who Died

Just as your personality is reflected in your grief, so too is the unique personality of the person who died. The way she talked, the way he smiled, the way she ate her food, the way he worked – all these and so many more little things go into creating personality. Whatever you loved most about the person who died, that is what you will now likely miss the most. And paradoxically, whatever you liked least about the person who died is what may trouble you the most now.

How would you describe the personality of the person who died?

Your Cultural Background

Your cultural background is an important part of how you experience and express your grief. When I say culture, I mean the values, rules (spoken or unspoken), and traditions that guide you and your family. Often, these values, rules, and traditions have been handed down generation after generation and are shaped by the ethnicities or regions of the world your family originally came from. Essentially, your culture is your way of being in the world.

What values and traditions have been passed on to you that may be influencing your grief?

Your Religious/Spiritual/Philosophical Background

Your personal belief systems can have a tremendous impact on your grief experience. You may discover that your religious/spiritual/philosophical life is deepened, renewed, or changed as a result of the death. Many people find themselves naturally questioning their beliefs as part of their work of mourning.

How has this death impacted your belief system?

Other Crises or Stresses in Your Life Right Now

What else is going on in your life right now? Although we often think it shouldn't, the earth does keep turning after the death of someone loved. You may still have other life and work obligations that demand your attention. And the more intense and numerous the other current stresses in your life, the more overwhelming your grief might be.

What other crises or stresses are part of your life right now and do you see them affecting your grief?

Your Experience with Loss and Death in the Past

Before this death, you may have experienced other significant losses in your life. In addition, other non-death losses in your past may also influence your grief. Divorce, job loss, financial downturns, severed relationships – all of these and more can affect your worldview as well as your current grief.

Have you had other significant losses (death and otherwise) in your life? If so, write them down and consider how they might be affecting your grief:

Your Physical and Mental Health

How you feel physically and mentally has a significant effect on your grief. If you are tired and eating poorly, your coping skills will be compromised. If you are dealing with physical or mental health issues before the death, this can naturally impact how you are coping with your grief.

Do you have any pre-existing or current physical or mental health challenges that are impacting your grief? If so, what are they?

Your Gender

Gender norms and social constructs may not only influence your grief but also the ways in which others relate to you at this time. Fortunately, as our culture's understanding of gender evolves, grieving people are getting to be grieving people – and that is as it should be. Your feelings are your feelings regardless of your gender.

Have gender expectations affected your grief and mourning? If so, how?

The Ritual or Funeral Experience

Funerals and other death-related ceremonies can have a major influence on your grief. Funerals are a time and a place to express your feelings about the death. The funeral also can serve as a time to honor the person who died, bring you closer to others who can give you needed support, affirm that life goes on even in the face of death, and give you a context of meaning that is keeping with your own religious, spiritual, or philosophical background. In short, a meaningful funeral can help put you on a good path to healing.

If you were unable to attend the funeral of the person who died, or if the funeral was minimized, distorted, or nonexistent, you may find that this complicates your grief experience.

Did you plan and/or attend a funeral service for the person who died? If so, describe what that experience was like for you:

Additional Influences on Your Grief and Mourning

What else has shaped your unique grief experience? There may well be other things you can reflect on large and small, that are influencing your grief right now. Make some notes about those things here:

As you create your GRIEF PLAN, awareness of the above influences will help you understand how your grief and mourning are experienced the way they are. For more in-depth discussion of these potential shapers of your grief, you may find it helpful to see my book, *Understanding Your Grief: Touchstones for Hope and Healing.*

WHAT YOU MAY FEEL IN YOUR GRIEF

"Emotions are a language. Every emotion means something. When you understand the language, you suddenly gain incredible insight into yourself and others."

- Scot Conway

Before you can create an action-oriented GRIEF PLAN, allow me to introduce you to some of the most common emotions that are experienced when grief touches our lives. As strange as some of the emotions might seem, they are a true expression of where you are on your grief journey at any given moment. Naming the feelings and acknowledging them are important steps toward eventually integrating them into your life.

Keep in mind, you may or may not experience each and every one of the emotions described below. Or you might move through one or more of these feelings, think you're "done" with it, then find yourself returning to it later on. Sometimes you may move from one predominant emotion to another in a short period of time. At other times, and perhaps more commonly, you may experience two or more emotions simultaneously.

As you read through these emotions, pay special attention to any in which you may feel "stuck." Feeling "stuck" is often an indication of where you need to give additional attention to the universal needs of mourning. I'll invite you to make some notes about each of the dimensions I describe and this will help you create your GRIEF PLAN.

Shock, Numbness, Denial, and Disbelief

You may feel dazed and stunned, especially during the time immediately following the death. You may also feel a sense of surrealness and distance from what is happening around you. Denial can also be common. These feelings are nature's way of protecting you from an overwhelming reality. You may experience heart palpitations, queasiness, stomach pains, or dizziness. You may also find yourself crying hysterically, screaming angrily, or even laughing.

While shock, numbness, denial, and disbelief can be helpful – even necessary – early in your grief, feeling "stuck" in them can block your path to healing.

Have these emotions been a part of your experience? If so, describe what this has been like for you and if you in any way feel "stuck":

Disorganization, Confusion, Searching, and Yearning

When we are in grief, we often feel distracted and befuddled. We may have trouble focusing or concentrating. We also sometimes search and yearn for the person who died. You might experience a sense of the person's presence or even have fleeting glimpses of them across the room. I call this latter experience, which is very common and normal, a "memory picture."

Have these emotions been a part of your experience? If so, describe what this has been like for you and if you in any way feel "stuck":

Anxiety, Panic, and Fear

As your head and heart begin to miss the person who died, you may naturally feel anxious. What happens after death? How will I go on? Little uncertainties arise as well. What will we do with the person's belongings? How will paperwork get completed? You may fear that you or others you love will die, too. You may even panic as you think through the repercussions of this death.

Have these emotions been a part of your experience? If so, describe what this has been like for you and if you in any way feel "stuck":

Explosive Emotions

Anger, hate, blame, terror, resentment, rage, and jealousy are common explosive emotions in grief. Such feelings are a form of protest. We instinctively don't want the death to be true. Our explosive emotions say, "No! This is NOT OK with me!" Underneath all these explosive emotions are usually feelings of helplessness, hurt, pain, and fear.

While explosive emotions are normal, they should moderate in intensity and duration as you do the work of mourning. Uncontrolled rage, self-harm, extreme risk-taking, harm to others, and harm to property are red flags signaling a need for professional help.

Have these emotions been a part of your experience? If so, describe what this has been like for you and if you in any way feel "stuck":

Guilt and Regret

Guilt, regret, and self-blame are common and natural feelings after the death of someone loved. You may have a case of the "if-onlys." "If only I had gotten him to the doctor sooner..." "If only I had been with her that night..." "If only I hadn't said..."

While these feelings of guilt or regret are natural, they are sometimes not logical to those around you. But remember – thinking is logical; feeling is not. Like all dimensions of grief, these emotions should soften over time as you allow yourself to mourn.

Have these emotions been a part of your experience? If so, describe what this has been like for you and if you in any way feel "stuck":

Sadness and Depression

Sadness and depression are often natural, authentic emotions after the death of someone loved. Someone precious in your life is no longer physically here. Of course you are sad. Of course you feel deep sorrow. Feeling your sadness is commonly a central part of allowing yourself to mourn. Sadness and depression naturally invite us to temporarily withdraw and regroup. When we are sad, we instinctively turn inward and slow down. This aids in your healing and provides time to begin to re-order your life.

For some grievers, the normal depression of grief can become debilitating enough to be classified as clinical depression. If you feel this may apply to you, please seek professional support.

Have these emotions been a part of your experience? If so, describe what this has been like for you and if you in any way feel "stuck":

Relief and Release

Sometimes you may feel a sense of relief or release when someone dies. This is especially common after extended illnesses or as a result of ambivalent relationships. Sometimes your feelings of relief can also make you feel guilty. "I shouldn't be feeling relieved," you may think. Relief-guilt may also arise when you recognize that you won't miss certain aspects of the relationship you had with the person who died. If you haven't allowed yourself to explore any potential feelings of relief and release, you may be at risk for feeling "stuck."

Have these emotions been a part of your experience? If so, describe what this has been like for you and if you in any way feel "stuck":

Physical Symptoms

You may also experience physiological changes as part of your grief. Actually, one literal definition of the word *grievous* is "causing physical suffering." Psyche and soma (body) often go together. You may be shocked by how much your body responds to the impact of your loss. Among the most common physical responses to loss are trouble with sleeping and low energy.

Muscle aches and pains, shortness of breath, feelings of emptiness in your stomach, tightness in your throat or chest, digestive problems, sensitivity to noise, heart palpitations, queasiness, nausea, headaches, increased allergic reactions, changes in appetite, weight loss or gain, agitation and generalized tension – are all ways your body may react to the loss of someone loved. It is always wise to get a general medical exam after experiencing a loss. However, if you find these physical symptoms persisting it may be an indication of the need to give more attention to your grief.

Have physical symptoms been a part of your experience? If so, describe what this has been like for you and if you in any way feel "stuck":

Additional Emotions You May Feel In Your Grief

What other emotions have you felt as part of your grief experience? Make some notes about those things here:

As you work to create your GRIEF PLAN your awareness of these emotions will be critical. They will provide the guidance you need to be able to integrate grief into your life. A normal and supportive way to experience feelings of grief is: feel them, acknowledge them, befriend them, share them, and finally have them witnessed and met with empathy by others. Creating your unique GRIEF PLAN will help you do just that!

For more in-depth discussion of these potential emotions, you may find it helpful to see my book, *Understanding Your Grief: Touchstones for Hope and Healing.*

CREATING YOUR GRIEF PLAN

THE SIX UNIVERSAL NEEDS OF MOURNING

"We must embrace the pain and burn it as fuel for our journey."

– Kenji Miyazawa

With the necessary backdrop of understanding the difference between grief and mourning, exploring the importance of hope, courage, and faith, reviewing the influences on your unique grief, and being introduced to what you may feel in your grief – it is time to create your GRIEF PLAN.

What is essential to helping you with your plan? The centerpiece is anchored in allowing yourself to mourn actively and openly – bit by bit, day by day. In other words, mourning a significant loss is a daily encounter. It is also a daily commitment.

I realize from my own experience that it can sometimes seem easier or less painful to keep grief inside of you. Yet ultimately, acknowledging and experiencing your pain inside of you while also sharing it outside of yourself is necessary for you to integrate it into your life. In other words, mourning is hard work. It takes time, energy, and attention.

How do you mourn? By creating an action plan to give attention to the six universal needs of mourning. While I have acknowledged that grief is intensely personal and unique, I long ago discovered that there are six universal needs that we all must befriend when someone in our life dies.

THE SIX UNIVERSAL NEEDS OF MOURNING

1. **Acknowledge the Reality of the Death**
   Gently confront the reality that someone you care about has died and will never physically be present in your life again.
2. **Embrace the Pain of the Loss**
   Recognize that the pain of grief is normal and necessary, and allow yourself to feel it fully when it arises.
3. **Remember the Person Who Died**
   Spend time recalling memories and sharing them with others.
4. **Develop a New Self-Identity**
   Consider anew who you are and what you want for yourself in the future.
5. **Search for Meaning**
   Question the purpose of life and find renewed meaning.
6. **Let Others Help You - Now and Always**
   Maintain and build relationships with others, both for grief support and for connection and companionship.

The power of these six needs of mourning is that while they are painful and difficult, they are also, over time, transformative. They will help you "hold your sorrow." They will give you the momentum you need to eventually not only survive, but to thrive.

Your awareness of these needs will help you take a participative, action-oriented approach to healing as opposed to thinking of grief as something you passively experience. You will be able to move toward your grief instead of away from it. I purposely used the word POWER in the title of this book. **Power in your grief journey means the capacity to shape and influence your unique experience.**

ESSENTIAL STEPS TO
WORKING YOUR GRIEF PLAN

"Goals are like a map. They help us determine where we want to end up, and give us personal direction on which to focus our energy."

- Catherine Pulsifer

As you prepare to befriend the six needs of mourning the following steps are critical to creating the divine momentum you need to eventually reconcile grief into your life.

Step 1: Set Your Intention

Recognizing that you must first set your intention is critical to ultimately being able to integrate grief into your life. When you set your intention to heal, you make a commitment to positively influence the course of your journey. Without this consciousness about doing what you need to do, there is a risk that you will end up feeling "stuck" in your grief.

Setting your intent allows you to choose between being a "passive witness" or an "active participant" in your grief. While your grief cannot be "fixed" or "resolved," it can and will be soothed through active engagement with and expressing your many thoughts and feelings.

Setting your intention to heal is not only a way of helping you survive your loss, it is also a way of guiding your grief to the most meaningful future. That is an excellent reason to give attention to your intention. The alternative would be to shut down in an effort to avoid and deny your pain, which is to risk dying while you are alive.

Write down your intentions here. What do you hope to achieve by working your GRIEF PLAN? What hopes do you have for your future?

Step 2: Acknowledge the Challenge

Actively participating in the hard work of mourning is naturally quite challenging. However, while difficult, you have the capacity to aid in your own healing. No, grief work does not happen quickly or efficiently. All change starts with chaos.

As a result, you must be patient with yourself. When you come to trust that the most intense pain will not last forever, it becomes tolerable. As you create your GRIEF PLAN, I will be encouraging you to gently befriend the pain of your grief. As you take on this challenge, trust that it will help you ultimately discover continued meaning and purpose in your life.

How do you feel about taking on this challenge? Write down any hesitations or concerns you may have about creating your GRIEF PLAN:

Step 3: Honor and Overcome Resistance

How did you feel when you read through Step 2? Did you feel yourself resisting the idea of acknowledging the challenge? If so, know that any resistance you might have is normal and natural.

Some people experiencing grief fear that if they start really focusing on and expressing their deepest thoughts and feelings, they may not be able to stop. Others are afraid of revealing to someone else what they feel inside or admitting to behaviors they feel ashamed of. At times, they worry that they are "not normal" or are "going crazy." And some are reluctant to befriend the pain of the loss because they see it as not serving a purpose. They may also lack an understanding of the role of hurt in healing. They might question "Why would I choose to befriend pain? It won't bring back the person who died."

Be assured that any resistance you may feel is normal. Notice the resistance, think of it trying to protect you, and then work to find ways to overcome it. As you work to create your GRIEF PLAN my hope is that you will have the courage, hope, and faith to work with any natural resistance you may be experiencing.

Allow yourself to acknowledge any resistance you may be feeling and write about it here:

Step 4: Seek and Accept Support

While you work on your GRIEF PLAN you need and deserve additional support. You will discover that the sixth need of mourning (see page 111) will encourage you to engage in activities related to seeking and accepting support. Yes, grief is, in part, a solitary activity because it happens inside you. But allow me to remind you that mourning is "the shared response to loss." We all need and deserve support when we have sorrows of the soul.

My hope is that you have family and friends who will listen with kindness and compassion should you want to share your GRIEF PLAN with them. Even if for whatever reason you don't want to share your detailed plan with them, simply having them nearby can help you feel loved and supported. If you don't have good social support, or if you are not able to open up to your family and friends, you will be well-served to seek additional outside support.

Even if you do have a good support system, I still want to encourage you to consider locating a compassionate grief-informed counselor to help support you as you work your GRIEF PLAN. I think adding a caring, trained grief counselor to your support team has the potential of being a tremendous help to you. Having a "responsibility partner" as you actively dose the six needs of mourning will be invaluable.

Take a few minutes to reflect on your support system and write about it here. Do you have family and friends that can be supportive to you as you actively mourn? Have you considered reaching out to a grief-informed counselor?

Step 5: Care for Yourself

As you actively work on your GRIEF PLAN it is critically important to give attention to your self-care. Over my 40-plus years of companioning people in grief, I have discovered that most of us are hard on ourselves when we are experiencing grief. We are at risk of judging ourselves and putting ourselves last. But excellent self-care is essential to being able to work your grief plan in ways that result in what I will go on to describe as **reconciliation**. To practice good self-care does not mean you are feeling sorry for yourself or being self-indulgent. Rather, it means you are creating conditions that allow you to integrate the death into your heart and soul.

In reality, self-care fortifies you for the naturally challenging grief journey, a journey that leaves you profoundly affected and deeply changed. To be self-nurturing is to have the courage to give focused attention to the six needs of mourning. When we recognize that grief care begins with ourselves, we no longer think of those around us as being responsible for our well-being. Healthy self-care allows you to mourn in ways that help you heal — and that is nurturing indeed.

How do you feel you are doing with your self-care? Write about it here:

Step 6: Work your GRIEF PLAN and allow yourself to authentically mourn

As I have previously noted, mourning is anything that involves expressing your grief outside of yourself in some way. It is giving attention to your grief via active, intentional engagement surrounding the six universal needs of mourning. The key is matching up the activities and practices that are an appropriate fit for you.

As you create your GRIEF PLAN you will be able to select the specific activities that will help you "dose" your need to authentically mourn. You will want to practice patience as you work your plan. Integrating grief is not something that can be done in a short period of time. That is why one of my favorite mantras is: "No rewards for speed." You cannot heal grief in a few days or weeks. Instead, you will be well-served to remember that active mourning will soften your grief, slowly in a wave-like fashion. But only if it is done in small, regular doses.

Understanding the Need to Dose Your Mourning

The good news is that you don't have to actively and intentionally express your grief for hours each day to begin to feel like you are making some movement. I believe it is so important to understand you cannot embrace the pain that comes with grief in one sitting. After all, if we as humans were to feel our life losses all at once, we could not survive.

Instead, you must invite yourself to "dose" your pain – to feel it in small waves then allow it to retreat until you are ready for the next wave. I call this back-and-forth of grief and respite "encounter-evade." You intentionally encounter your grief for a while, then you evade it until you are ready to encounter it again.

Of course, you will not be able to completely escape your pain. Even when you are not giving it your full attention, it will be there in the background. Your grief may forcefully break through at times when least expected. I call this a "griefburst" – a sudden, sharp feeling of grief that naturally causes anxiety and a heightened sense of loss.

Again, you cannot and should not expect yourself to give the pain of grief your full attention all the time. Befriending pain is fatiguing, difficult work, so it is absolutely essential to replenish your energy as often and as fully as you can.

WHAT IS HEALING IN GRIEF?

I have noted that bereavement means "to be torn apart." To heal in grief means "to become whole again." It means to integrate your grief into yourself and to learn to continue your changed life with fullness and meaning. To be able to experience a new and changed "wholeness" requires that you engage in the work of mourning. It does not just happen to you. To heal you must actively attend to and express that which has broken you. Note that healing is not the same as "curing," which is a medical term that means "remedying" or "correcting." You cannot remedy your grief, but you can reconcile it. You cannot correct your grief, but you can heal it. For more on reconciliation, see page 127.

UNDERSTANDING AND ENGAGING IN THE SIX UNIVERSAL NEEDS OF MOURNING

"I knew that running from the darkness would only lead to greater darkness later on. I learned to live and mourn simultaneously."

– Gerald L. Sittser

MOURNING NEED 1: Acknowledge the reality of the death	**MOURNING NEED 2:** Embrace the pain of the loss	**MOURNING NEED 3:** Remember the person who died
MOURNING NEED 4: Develop a new self-identity	**MOURNING NEED 5:** Search for meaning	**MOURNING NEED 6:** Let others help you—now and always

From my own experiences with loss as well as those of the thousands of grieving people I have companioned over the years, I have learned that if we are to heal, we cannot skirt the outside edges of our grief. Instead, we must journey all through it, sometimes meandering the side roads, sometimes plowing directly into its raw center. An essential part of developing your GRIEF PLAN is to familiarize yourself with what I call the "six universal needs of mourning." Your awareness of these needs will invite you to actively participate in the work of mourning.

You will note that the needs are numbered one through six. This is not meant to imply that your grief journey will be an orderly procession toward healing. These needs of mourning are not "stages." If you are like most mourners, you will encounter the needs of mourning in random fashion. What's more, you will likely find yourself working on more than one need at a time.

As I describe each of the six needs to you, I will also introduce **signals** that might suggest some inhibition of each need. Some people might use the word symptoms – but I prefer the term signals to get out of the medical model of mental health care. I will also present questions to ask yourself about each need, and then most importantly, provide you with potential activities that can help you actively engage in each of the needs of mourning. My intent is to invite you to have insight into what you can do as you help yourself actively and authentically mourn.

My sincere hope is to create some divine momentum for you – by that I mean creating experiences for you to be propelled toward healing by doing what is necessary and helpful to you. As you make use of the activities that are an appropriate match for your unique needs, you probably will notice that you feel a bubble of hope or are buoyed by a sense of movement toward reconciliation. In other words, you will feel a little better and a little more hopeful about the future. This is the power of divine momentum.

Mourning Need 1: Acknowledge the Reality of the Death

"While embracing the reality of this death is painful beyond words, the more I open myself to allowing small doses of reality in, the more I open my heart to healing."

– The Journey Through Grief

MOURNING NEED 1:

Acknowledge the reality of the death

Have you ever noticed that you can know something in your head before you know it in your heart? This is often what happens when someone we love dies. This need of mourning, what I often refer to as the linchpin need, involves gently confronting and acknowledging the reality that someone you care about will never physically be back in your life again. The reason I refer to this as the linchpin need of mourning is because if you don't fully acknowledge the reality of the death, it naturally results in an inhibition of the other five needs.

Whether the death was sudden or anticipated, acknowledging the full reality of the death can take weeks, months, sometimes even years. You may expect him or her to come through the door, to call on the telephone, or even to reach out and touch you. At times, it is instinctive to try to push away the reality of the death. It is part of what I referred to earlier as the movement between encounter-evade.

Again, it is not unusual or abnormal to move back and forth between protesting and encountering the reality of the death. Some of the activities I will invite you to consider as part of your GRIEF PLAN will help you replay events surrounding the death and confront memories, both good and bad. This replay or re-telling of the story of the death is a vital part of this need of mourning. It is as if each time you talk about it, the reality of the death becomes a little more real.

One moment the reality of the death may be tolerable and another moment it may be intolerable. At times you may feel like running away and hiding. At other times, you may hope you will wake up from a dream and he or she will still be alive.

I sometimes discover that a griever is acknowledging some of the reality of the death but not all realities of the death. For example, they may acknowledge that someone in their life has died, but they may not fully acknowledge the cause of the death or some of the circumstances surrounding it. Yet, for grief to become authentic mourning, we as humans are faced with the need to eventually fully acknowledge the death as well as the circumstances.

Specific circumstances of the death can be particularly hard to fathom (such as suicide, homicide, unexpected traumatic death, or when a body is unrecoverable). This is also true when there was an extremely close relationship, when a funeral was not held, the body was not viewable, or cultural, religious, or family system influences shut down any open discussion of the death. We as humans are capable of coping with what we know, but we cannot cope with what we do not know or are hiding from ourselves.

So, I encourage you to remind yourself that it is normal to move back and forth between evading and encountering the reality of the death. However, if you get stuck in any form of longer-term denial it can put you at risk for grieving but not mourning. The activities I will go on to propose are intended to help you be self-compassionate if you determine you need more engagement with this linchpin need.

Signals That Suggest Potential Inhibition of This Need

In my experience, the primary signals that invite more attention to this need include – but are not limited to – the following: extended shock, denial, anxiety, depression, disorganization, and confusion.

What in the beginning served you well as a normal, temporary "time-out" from a harsh reality may have become stuck or fixed. These signals may have now persisted in ways that have stalled the active process of grief and mourning.

I have sometimes found that grievers who are denying or repressing the full reality of the death are unconsciously trying to reverse the death or "hold on" to the person who died. In part, to do this is instinctive and you would not want to shame yourself if you can relate to this as part of your experience. After all, if you don't engage with the reality, you can hope that your heart will whisper to you, "Maybe it isn't real." As hard as it is, it is in giving yourself permission to convert your grief into active mourning that helps shift the nature of the bonds.

Another discovery in my counseling experience is that in addition to shock and denial, the inability or refusal to acknowledge the reality of the death may lead to risk for anxiety, depression, forms of self-punishment by not caring for oneself, and/or generalized anger. Some people are also at risk for trying to self-treat their pain in ways that inhibit the ability to acknowledge the full reality of the death. This can result when there is a pattern of alcohol or drug abuse, premature involvement in new relationships, overeating, or impulsive spending.

Another signal I at times witness when there is an inhibition of this need is pronounced or prolonged disorganization and confusion. Muddled cognition is often symptomatic of a mind and heart that have not completely come to terms with the new reality.

There can also be circumstances where you simply don't feel safe to be able to initiate a genuine encounter with this need. This is common in circumstances of traumatic death (sudden, unexpected, and/or calamitous). Processing the traumatic elements is often necessary before the reality of the death itself can be approached and engaged with. This may require you to seek professional help to do what is called "trauma processing" before grief more organically converts to active mourning.

Practical considerations can also contribute to an inhibition of this need being met. For example, having a stable and secure living situation and adequate financial support are prerequisites to effective grief support. Unstable living conditions naturally complicate the ability to actively mourn. It is difficult to dose the six needs of mourning when basic needs are unable to be met.

Again, I consider this to be the linchpin mourning need. Why? Because until you actively acknowledge the full reality of the death, the other mourning needs are largely blocked. Until this need is effectively encountered, the other needs are either inhibited completely or touched on shallowly or ineffectively.

Questions to Ask Yourself:

These questions are intended to help you see where you are in "dosing" this need. Overall, how do you see yourself doing on acknowledging the reality of the death?

What experiences and activities have you engaged in since the death that have helped you acknowledge the reality?

Are there any circumstances around the death or the nature of your relationship that have naturally complicated this need for you?

Acknowledging the death with your head is different than acknowledging it with your heart. How is your heart doing on acknowledging the reality?

Can you identify anything specific that makes it challenging to acknowledge the reality?

Do you have any unanswered questions or concerns that might be hindering your ability to acknowledge the reality? If so, what are they?

Have you had any tendencies to numb yourself from the reality in any self-destructive ways such as alcohol or drug abuse, premature involvement in new relationships, overeating, or impulsive spending? If so, what have you done that might not ultimately be helpful to you?

Active Engagement With Mourning Need 1:

You may have discovered you would benefit from more active dosing of this need. If so, review the below activities and note which ones may be helpful to you as you create your GRIEF PLAN.

1. RE-TELL YOUR STORY

An important place to start with any inhibition of this need is to tell the story of the life and death of the person who died. An essential part of healing grief is often "telling the story" over and over again. Frequently the areas you need to give backward attention to are the nature of the relationship you had and the circumstances around the death. Yes, it is normal and necessary to revisit these critical influences on your grief. The more you tell it, the more it starts to come together into a coherent narrative with a beginning, a middle, and an end. The more you tell it, the deeper your acknowledgment of the loss becomes, and the more you begin to discover a level of understanding of what happened. It is when you acknowledge in both your head and heart that your precious person has died and that you cannot change that reality that your authentic mourning begins.

The key is to find compassionate people who are willing to listen to you tell your story over and over again. But remember that not everyone has the capacity to be an empathetic listener. So be sure to seek out listeners (caring friends or a grief-informed counselor) who can be present to your pain and understand your need to repeat the story. Remember – as you retell your story you are helping the internal grief become external mourning and creating divine momentum.

On a piece of paper, write down the names of three people who can be supportive to you. Reach out to one of those people today. Ask if you can get together (either in person or over the phone) to tell them the story of the life and death of the person who died. As you tell your story, give focused attention to the nature of your relationship and the circumstances of the death.

2. WRITE IT OUT

Are you someone who likes to journal? Do you find yourself naturally writing about your thoughts and feelings? If so, lean into this inclination. Write out your understanding of the death and its impact on you. Let the words flow out of you and write as much or as little as you want. This activity will help you move from head understanding of the death to heart understanding. Even if you aren't someone who is naturally drawn to journaling, perhaps give it a try as a way to express your grief into mourning.

3. EXPLORE WHAT YOU DON'T KNOW ABOUT THE DEATH

Do you lack an understanding of the cause or circumstances of the death? Are there details surrounding the death that you would like to better understand? As you move from head to heart understanding, it can be helpful to reflect on what you do or do not know about the death. Ask yourself: Is there information I can seek out to help me better understand the circumstances around the death?

On a pad of paper write down all the questions you have about the circumstances of the death. Circle any where you might be able to seek the answers. If there are questions you may never fully understand but that are weighing on you, consider bringing them with you to see a grief-informed counselor.

4. SPEND TIME WITH YOUR LINKING OBJECTS

Linking objects are items that belonged to or connect you with the person who died. Things such as pictures, clothing, books, knick-knacks, jewelry, and other prized possessions can not only help you remember the person who died but also acknowledge their death.

After someone dies, people sometimes hurry into clearing out all the "stuff" because they think it will help them feel better. It usually doesn't. In fact, getting rid of the belongings because they're too painful to have around is antithetical to integrating the loss into your life. Acknowledging the reality of the death may include embracing the feelings that are stirred up by the belongings of the person who died. If you get rid of belongings prematurely, you may later find yourself wishing that you had some of them back. So, a simple reminder to go slow.

Find a linking object of the person who died and spend five uninterrupted minutes focusing on it. Touch it, smell it, close your eyes and remember the way the person who died wore or used it – pour all your energy into focusing on this object. As you do so, consider how you are saying hello on the path to goodbye.

5. WHAT DO YOU MISS?

With a trusted friend or counselor talk about what it is like to be in this world without the person who died. Explore what to do with the love or other feelings you have now that the person who died is no longer here. What is a day in your life like now in contrast to what it was like before the person died? What are three characteristics they had that you admired? What was that thing they always said? What is something they did that you now miss? If you could spend one more afternoon with them, what would you do?

As you explore these questions be self-compassionate and make sure you feel the support from your friend or counselor. Why? Because a wide range of emotions can naturally surface when you do this.

6. PLAN AND PARTICIPATE IN A MEANINGFUL CEREMONY

One of the many reasons we have ceremonies after death is to help us acknowledge the reality that someone died. Ceremonies help provide a structure to help us dose our need to let grief become mourning. They help us say hello to the reality that someone is no longer here physically.

If you did not have a funeral at the time of the death, it can be helpful to have additional ceremonies. Even if you did have a meaningful funeral, you can never have too many ceremonies. Consider creating a ceremony or even a series of ceremonies that build in the function of revisiting the reality of the death. As I often say, "When words are inadequate, have ceremony."

Consider this simple candle-lighting ceremony as a starting point:

In this ceremony, lit candles represent your ongoing love for the person who died. Gather a group of people who are also grieving this death and invite them to sit in a circle. Let everyone know that they will be invited to share a memory of the person who died and remind them that it is OK to be vulnerable and authentic. Pass out unlit candles so that everyone has one.

You will go first. Light your candle and say, "We are here today to honor our love and memories, which never die. My love for ______________ (name of person) is a flame I carry inside me." Now share something you loved and miss about the person who died. It might be a quality of this person or an anecdote. Or it might be something you have been struggling with as you try to find ways to live without this person. When you are finished, turn to the person next to you and say, "Your love for ____________ (name of person) is a flame you carry inside you." Use your lit candle to light this person's candle. Now it is their turn to share a thought or memory, then pass the flame on to the person next to them, saying, "Your love for ____________ (name of person) is a flame you carry inside you." Continue going around the circle until everyone has shared. At the end, everyone's candles should be lit. Consider closing the ceremony with a reading, prayer, or piece of music.

For additional ideas on how to plan and carry out ceremonies, see my book *Grief Day by Day: Simple Practices to Help You Survive... and Thrive.*

GRIEF PLAN for Need 1:

Write down below the activities you think you can make use of as part of your GRIEF PLAN. Also write out any additional ideas you have that you think might help you dose this need of mourning.

____

____

____

____

____

____

____

____

____

____

Mourning Need 2: Embrace the Pain of the Loss

"I don't have to go in search of the pain of grief – it finds me. It's when I deny or insulate myself from the pain of the loss that I shut down. Ironically, it is in being open to the pain that I move through it to renewed living."

– The Journey Through Grief

MOURNING NEED 2:
Embrace the pain of the loss

This need of mourning is all about learning to befriend the pain of your grief – something you may not naturally want to do. After all, it is easier to avoid, repress, or deny the pain of grief than it is to greet it head-on. Yet, it is in confronting our pain that we eventually integrate it into our lives.

I'm often asked what I mean by "embracing" the pain of grief as it seems almost antagonistic. I also like to use the verb "befriending" and people ask about that term as well. When I say that this need of mourning is to embrace your pain, I'm first asking you to acknowledge the appropriateness of the pain. Someone you love – someone who gave your life meaning – has died. Of course it hurts! Of course you feel pain! Where there was love or attachment, there will naturally be pain when a death occurs.

There is a critical difference between "coping" and "embracing." If we're coping, we are just getting by. If we're embracing, we are turning toward our grief and befriending it.

So in addition to emphasizing that you must recognize your pain as normal, I'm further suggesting that over time you need to learn to look upon your pain as a reflection of your love. As you probably realize, love and grief are two sides of the same precious coin. If your love is good and valuable, so, too, is your grief. And like your love, it will require your loving attention as you allow yourself to mourn.

Even so, you will discover that you need to dose yourself as you embrace your pain. We've discussed this already, but here's a reminder: you cannot (nor should you try to) overload yourself with the hurt all at one time. Sometimes you may need to distract yourself from the pain of your grief, while at other times you will need to create a safe place to move toward it.

Feeling your pain can sometimes zap you of your energy. When your energy is low you may be tempted to suppress your grief or even run from it. If you start running and keep running, you may never heal. Dose your pain: Yes! Deny your pain: No!

Unfortunately, as I have said, our culture tends to encourage the denial of pain. We often misunderstand the role of hurt, pain, and suffering. If you openly express your feelings of grief, misinformed friends may advise you to "carry on" or "keep your chin up." If, on the other hand, you remain "strong" and "in control," you may be congratulated for "doing well" with your grief. Actually, doing well with your grief means becoming well acquainted with your pain. Don't let others deny you this critical mourning need.

Embracing the pain of grief is a vital part of active, authentic mourning. You will befriend your pain by sitting with it, being present to it, thinking about it, and feeling it. But to convert grief into mourning, you must express it outside of yourself regularly. People who listen without judgment are your most important helpers as you work on this mourning need.

As you create your GRIEF PLAN keep in mind that grief requires convalescence: something that by its nature is slow and recursive. Your pain will probably ebb and flow. Embracing it when it washes over you will require hope, courage, and faith.

Signals That Suggest Potential Inhibition of This Need

In my experience, the primary signals that invite more attention to this need include – but are not limited to – the following: anxiety, panic, fear, explosive emotions, sadness, and depression.

The opposite of embracing or befriending pain can be reflected in attempts to exert control over the uncontrollable. Underlying this controlling impulse is fear that results in anxiety – the fear that you cannot tolerate the pain of the loss. In fact, for some people this anxiety evolves to the point of panic attacks.

For some people there is a lack of awareness that the fear of the pain can result in projecting their anxiety onto other, seemingly unrelated concerns. If this fits for you, you may find you are anxious about various things going on in your life or experience a generalized anxiety. However, the real source of your anxiety can potentially be that you are not giving enough attention to the pain of your loss.

Explosive emotions are another constellation of signals I observe when there is an inhibition surrounding the pain that comes with the loss. Feelings such as anger, hate, blame, terror, resentment, rage, and jealousy sometimes serve as defense mechanisms against hurt and vulnerability. What's more, explosive emotions may push supportive family members and friends away. This can be an unconscious way to stay safe from the pain you may feel when you open up to others.

I also find that some grievers who report being depressed are sometimes unaware that their depression is tied to a lack of engagement with the pain of the loss. Just because you may feel deeply sad or depressed does not always mean you are authentically encountering the pain of your grief. In fact, you may describe feeling sad and/or "empty" but may not think there is any value in befriending your pain. The result can be risk for a chronic, low-grade depression, which could be softened by more intentional engagement with your hurt, pain, and suffering.

Questions to Ask Yourself:

These questions are intended to help you see where you are in "dosing" this need. Overall, how do you see yourself doing on embracing the pain of the loss?

What experiences and activities have you engaged in since the death that have helped you encounter and express the pain?

What has been most painful for you about the death and why?

Has the intensity of your pain changed since the death? If so, how? If not, why do you think that might be?

Where do you see yourself having trouble when it comes to embracing the pain of the loss?

Are there parts of the pain that you have mostly been keeping inside yourself? If so, what are they?

Active Engagement With Mourning Need 2:

You may have discovered you would benefit from more active dosing of this need. If so, review the below activities and note which ones may be helpful to you as you create your GRIEF PLAN.

1. SIT WITH YOUR PAIN

You can befriend your pain by sitting with it, being present to it, thinking about it, and truly feeling it. Attempts to avoid, repress, or deny the pain make you an opponent to your journey and hinders your capacity to integrate the loss. Many people in grief keep busy so they don't have to feel and pay attention to their pain. They think if they ignore it long enough, it will go away. It doesn't. Remember, to feel it is to heal it.

To sit with your pain, you must stop doing and talking and start being and listening. Find a quiet space where you can be free from distractions. As you sit down, scan your body for discomfort and relax any tense muscles. Focus on the pain of your grief, especially any feelings or thoughts that you may have been trying to deny. As painful thoughts and feelings arise, give them your non-judgmental attention. After a few minutes of experiencing your pain, allow yourself to go about your day. Repeat this activity 2-3 times a week. Occasionally sitting with your pain allows you to actively dose it and befriend it.

2. REFRAME YOUR PAIN

You may be at risk for thinking that experiencing pain means you are not making movement in your grief. Yet, it is in allowing yourself to befriend the pain that actually helps soften the pain. In other words, the pain you are experiencing is appropriate and functional. It is naturally present for a reason. It is not only normal, it is necessary.

To reframe your pain it may be helpful to actively think of it as a friend you can reach out to. Either electronically or with pen and paper, write a letter to your pain. Start it with, "Dear Pain, ..." Try to write as if you were writing to a friend. Use casual and familiar language. Tell the pain what you want it to know about you and your relationship with the person who died. Try to give the pain grace. Tell it you will write again when you can.

3. INVENTORY YOUR PAINFUL SIGNALS

You have probably experienced lots of different grief signals since the death occurred. Grief is like that. It's composed of a wide range of thoughts and feelings, and it tends to shift, change, and circle back on itself from day to day, week to week, and month to month.

I have outlined a list below of some of the common signals that people share with me. I invite you to circle those you have encountered since your loss, then put a star next to any you are feeling most strongly today. If any of your signals are not on the list, please add them in the spot marked "other."

COMMON GRIEF FEELINGS

Since my loss, I've felt...

Abandoned
Afraid
Angry
Anxious
Ashamed
Betrayed
Bewildered
Bitter
Blameful
Confused
Crazy
Crushed
Defeated
Depressed
Desolate
Desperate
Devastated
Disbelieving
Disgusted
Disorganized
Distraught
Embarrassed
Empty
Encouraged
Envious
Fearful
Fed up
Flustered
Fragmented
Frantic
Frightened
Frustrated
Furious
Guilty
Happy
Hateful
Helpless
Hopeless
Horrified
Hurt
Irritable
Jealous
Joyful
Judgmental
Lonely

Lost
Loveless
Mad
Numb
OK
Overwhelmed
Panicked
Powerless
Rageful
Regretful
Relieved
Resentful
Sad
Scared
Shocked
Stunned
Surprised
Terrified
Terrorized
Trapped
Unwanted
Weak
Worried
Worthless
Yearnful
Zoned out

Other:

____

____

____

____

____

____

____

Now you have the opportunity to feel and spend time with your signals. We as humans can be pretty good at ignoring or distracting ourselves from our painful thoughts and feelings. Yet, you have them for a good reason — someone in your life has died.

Pick one of the feelings you starred — perhaps one you are really experiencing today. You have identified the feeling. You have normalized the feeling. What thoughts are you having that are associated with this feeling? What memories do you have that you associate with the loss related to this feeling?

Next, sit with this feeling for a while. Feel it in your body. Think it with your thoughts. Experience it with your memories. Try to place your awareness on nothing but this feeling for at least five to ten minutes. Yes, this can be challenging, but it can and will help you dose this need.

4. EXPLORE THE RULES YOU LEARNED ABOUT BEFRIENDING PAIN IN YOUR FAMILY OF ORIGIN

Sometimes your struggle to befriend pain can be anchored in your family of origin. For example, as a child you may have learned that you were not allowed to express your anger. If you did, you may have been sent to your room or punished. Now, even as an adult, when you may need to appropriately acknowledge and express explosive emotions, you may have trouble doing so.

You may now be faced with the need to try to rewrite the family "rules" you learned from a tender age. This requires that you recognize, befriend, and integrate all of your inner thoughts and feelings. This activity invites you to give thought to what rules existed in your family of origin about any feelings of grief. Could you express what you were feeling at times of loss? Or did you grow up in what is called a "closed family system" that discouraged or denied your need to befriend your feelings?

Inventory and write out a list of any "grief rules" that existed in your family of origin. Take this list to a trusted friend or grief-informed counselor to discuss how they may still be influencing you to this day.

5. MOVE YOUR BODY

Feelings of grief are often contained in the body as well as the head and heart. Keep in mind that your use of physical activities such as painting, drawing, and exercising are avenues through which you can express your feelings. Select an activity that requires you to move your body. Devote some time to this activity today.

Consciously reflect on how you feel before, during, and after the activity. Does your grief feel different in your body?

Some additional options might include planting a memorial garden, sewing a quilt, or participating in a memory walk. Do whatever speaks to your interests and personality. I have found that any activity that allows for physical movement may at times help you even more than verbal expression alone.

6. DISPLAY A SYMBOL OF YOUR GRIEF

In centuries past, mourners identified themselves in some way to communicate that they were "torn apart" and experiencing the normal pain of grief. Wearing jewelry, displaying wreaths, or keeping locks of hair from the person who died were common practices. Black clothing, or mourning clothes, were worn for a set period of time. Sometimes mourners wore armbands or buttons.

These kinds of mourning symbols unite us in our times of grief and convey the important message: "Someone in my life has died. I would appreciate your support, compassion, and understanding." My Center for Loss and Life Transition provides those who visit pins that read: Under Reconstruction.

Locate or create some form of a symbol that you can wear that allows you to acknowledge your feelings of loss. This visual reminder will often activate support from people around you. And remember— never apologize for making use of symbols to acknowledge you are experiencing grief. After all, if you were to apologize, you would be dismissing your truth.

GRIEF PLAN for Need 2:

Write down below the activities you think you can make use of as part of your GRIEF PLAN. Also write out any additional ideas you have that you think might help you dose this need of mourning.

Mourning Need 3: Remember the Person Who Died

"Remembering the person I have loved allows me to slowly heal. Healing does not mean I will forget. Actually, it means I will remember. Gently, I will move forward, never forgetting my past."

– The Journey Through Grief

MOURNING NEED 3:
Remember the person who died

Do you have any kind of relationship with someone after they die? Of course. You have a relationship of memory. Precious memories, dreams reflecting the significance of the relationship, and objects that link you to the person who died (such as photos, souvenirs, clothing, etc.) are examples of some of the things that give testimony to a different form of a continued relationship. This need of mourning involves allowing and encouraging yourself to pursue this relationship of memory.

Embracing your memories can be a very slow and, at times, painful process that occurs in small steps. Remember – don't try to do all your work of mourning at once. Go slowly and be patient with yourself.

Some people may try to take your memories away. Trying to be helpful, they might encourage you to take down photos of the person who died. They may tell you to keep busy or that you would be better off to move out of your house. You, too, might think avoiding memories would be better for you. And why not? You are living in a culture that teaches you to move away from your grief, instead of toward it.

Our culture may be encouraging you to move on, but one of the paradoxes of grief is that you must go backward before you can go forward. Grief by its very nature is a recursive process. That means it curves and spirals back on itself. It's repetitive. It covers the same ground more than once. Usually it is not even a two-steps-forward, one-step-backward kind of journey. Instead, it's often a one-step-forward, two-steps-in-a-circle, one-step-backward process. It takes time, patience, and yes, lots of backward motion before forward motion predominates.

When you actively remember the person who died, you go backward. When you tell the story of your love and loss from the beginning, you go backward. When you think back to earlier losses in your life and how they may be affecting your current grief, you go backward. When you work on your self-identity and think back to old interests you may now want to revisit, you go backward. These and other backward-looking experiences are a normal and necessary part of grief.

So go backward as much and as often as you need to. As long as you are actively engaging with your grief, you can trust that one day you will look up and find that you have indeed moved forward in meaningful ways. In my experience it is in remembering the past that makes hoping for the future possible. Your future will become open to new experiences only to the extent that you embrace the past.

Signals That Suggest Potential Inhibition of This Need

In my experience, the primary signals that invite more attention to this need include – but are not limited to – the following: disorganization, confusion, explosive emotions, guilt, sadness, and depression.

I sometimes discover that disorientation and confusion signal the need to engage in more memory work. Often called "brain fog", this comes across as scatteredness, an incapacity to focus, and/or an inability to accomplish the tasks of daily living. When you inhibit or push aside memories, you are at risk for being unable to focus on anything else. When you suppress or deny the need for memory work, disorientation will harden instead of soften. This can relate to fear of fully acknowledging the reality of the death and the pain that results when doing so.

Explosive emotions may also be symptomatic of an inhibition of this mourning need. For example, if the person in your life died suddenly or unexpectedly you may be naturally challenged to recall the event of the death. In addition, it can make it more challenging to access earlier memories, both good and bad. For a time it can just be too painful to remember. Your explosive emotions can be ways of instinctively defending against underlying feelings of helplessness, hurt, pain, and suffering. As with needs one and two, authentic befriending of need three will almost always help soften explosive emotions.

Signals of guilt and regret may also be tied to an insufficient encounter with need three. Feelings of guilt tend to stem from one or a handful of memories. It is human nature to focus on times in a relationship we wish would have gone differently – these "if only I would have..." "Why didn't I..." or "I should have..." regrets. To be able to shift your relationship from presence to memory requires that you encounter memories that reflect your entire relationship. Exploring memories of all points of the relationship – from the happiest to the most challenging – will help you put any regrettable moments into context. Your relationship with someone cannot be defined by a single moment in time. Allowing yourself to reflect on a wide range of memories will help you embrace this important need.

The signals of pronounced sadness and depression can also be an indication of the need for more dosing of this need. For example, if you experienced a sudden, unexpected death you may feel stuck on circumstances surrounding the death and need help in slowly and gently recalling memories of the relationship. Being able to do memory work can help transform despair into hope. Active remembering can be difficult and sometimes very painful. Yet, finding safe people and safe places to openly share memories will often eventually result in your smiling through tears. Your feelings of sadness and depression can then, and only then, begin to soften through active and ongoing memory work.

Questions to Ask Yourself:

These questions are intended to help you see where you are in "dosing" this need. Overall, how do you see yourself doing on remembering the person who died?

What experiences and activities have you engaged in since the death that have helped you encounter and remember the person who died?

What do you miss the most about the person who died?

What do you miss the least about the person who died?

Have you or have you not been able to share memories of the person who died? Explain here...

Things the person used to say were...

What was one of the most important qualities you liked about the person who died?

What was a time the person who died encouraged or uplifted you?

Active Engagement With Mourning Need 3:

You may have discovered you would benefit from more active dosing of this need. If so, review the below activities and note which ones may be helpful to you as you create your GRIEF PLAN.

1. GO BACKWARD

With the "buck up," "move forward," "put the past in the past" messages our culture tends to project, you are naturally at risk for trying to push forward in absence of the backward reflection that is necessary. Doing your memory work is just that – work. Remember – you must listen to the music of the past, so you can sing in the present, and dance into the future!

For some people, grief support groups, where people come together and share the common bond of having experienced a loss, can be invaluable in helping them go backward. In these groups, each person can share their unique grief journey in a non-threatening, safe atmosphere. Group leaders and members are usually very patient with you and your grief and understand your need for support long after the death.

If you have not joined a support group but are willing to consider it, take the steps to find a group today. You can start as simply as googling "grief support groups in my area." You can also reach out to local funeral homes, hospices, and faith communities to see if they offer groups. Online or virtual support groups are increasingly available and may also be an option for you.

2. USE THE NAME OF THE PERSON WHO DIED

As humans, we naturally love to hear the names of our loved ones. Yet, after someone dies, an all-too-common reaction is to stop using their name. It is as if we, or the people around us, think that if we don't use the name we won't be reminded about the death. But not using the name doesn't spare us from our grief, and it can create a false pretense where we avoid talking about the person at all. So, yes, use the person's name and encourage those around you to as well. Doing so is a reflection that love doesn't end with death.

If you find yourself hesitating to use the name of the person who died, it may be helpful to keep with you a conscious reminder to do so. This can be a piece of clothing or jewelry that you wear, or a small item that you keep in your pocket. Whenever you touch or interact with this item, remind yourself of your love for the person and to use their name. I remember when _________ ...," or "I was of thinking of ________ today because..."

3. REVIEW YOUR RELATIONSHIP

On a piece of paper, draw a long, straight line with hash marks on both ends. Take time to do a comprehensive review of your relationship on this timeline – starting from the time they entered your life until they died. Include any major events in your relationship with them. Below the timeline, describe the nature of the connection you had – good times, hard times, specific challenges, mutual interests and values, etc.

Explore the various emotions that may evolve for you from this relationship review. Doing this activity does not in any way mean you are "letting go," it just helps you appropriately shift the relationship from presence to memory.

4. GIVE FOCUSED ATTENTION TO ANY UNPLEASANT MEMORIES

We need to acknowledge that memories are not always pleasant. If this applies to you, this need of mourning can be even more difficult, and an inhibition can potentially take place. To ignore or deny any painful and ambivalent memories will prevent healing from taking place. If you repress or deny these memories, you also risk carrying the inhibited signals (disorganization, confusion, explosive emotions, guilt, sadness, and depression) into the future.

Think about your relationship with the person who died. Do you have unpleasant memories you have been trying to deny? If so, the best thing you can do is talk about them with a compassionate listener. However, if your memories are particularly challenging or traumatic, your friends and family may be unable to provide the support you need. Consider making an appointment with a grief-informed counselor who is trained to help you with this challenging memory work.

5. ORGANIZE A MOURNING BOOK

Perhaps one of the best ways to embrace memories is through creating a "memory book" that contains special photographs you have selected and perhaps other memorabilia such as ticket stubs, cards, etc. If available, also consider including things like a birth certificate, schoolwork, newspaper clippings, locks of hair, old letters, or copies of emails. Organize these items, place them in an album, and write out the memories reflected in them. If you would like, contact others who knew the person who died and ask them to write a note or contribute photos. This book can then become a valued collection of memories that you can review whenever you so desire.

The act of creating a memory book is mourning. Showing it to others and talking about it is, too. Other ideas might be: putting together a memory box, creating photo buttons, or sewing together a memory quilt.

6. GIVE ATTENTION TO ANY "UNFINISHED BUSINESS"

It is not unusual for there to be aspects of unfinished business in your relationship with someone who has died. Perhaps there were things you always wanted to say to them, things the two of you wanted to do, or places you wanted to go together. Or perhaps there had been conflict or ambivalence in your relationship that you were never able to resolve. If you can relate to this, it is important to give yourself permission to give this some focused attention. When there is unfinished business there continues to be an emotional attachment that needs to be mourned openly and honestly.

With a pad and paper write the person who died a letter. Tell them what is on your mind and heart. Include anything you wish you had said to them when they were alive. After you are done with your letter put it in an envelope and put it aside for at least a few days. When you do return, re-read the letter and imagine that the person who died could write a letter responding to you. What do you think they would say? Write out their response to you. If it is helpful to you, respond to them. Continue this imaginary dialogue for as long as you want, exploring any aspects of "unfinished business" you feel there is in your relationship.

GRIEF PLAN for Need 3:

Write down below the activities you think you can make use of as part of your GRIEF PLAN. Also write out any additional ideas you have that you think might help you dose this need of mourning.

Mourning Need 4: Develop a New Self-Identity

"My grief journey opens me to every level of my identity. The loss of a mirror to who I am invites me to acknowledge my transformation. The more I come to understand the new me, the more I have to give back to my life and to those I love."

– The Journey Through Grief

MOURNING NEED 4:
Develop a new self-identity

This need of mourning is about your personal identity, or self-perception, and is the result of the ongoing process of establishing who you are following the death.

Part of your self-identity comes from the relationships you have with other people. When someone with whom you have a relationship dies, your self-identity, or the way you see yourself, naturally changes.

You may have gone from being a "wife" or "husband" to a "widow" or "widower." You may have gone from being a "parent" to a "bereaved parent." The way you define yourself and the way society defines you changes. As one woman told me, "I used to have a husband and was part of a couple. Now I'm not only single, but a single parent and a widow… I hate that word. It makes me sound like a lonely spider."

What's more, a death often requires you to take on new roles that had been filled by the person who died. After all, someone still has to take out the garbage, someone still has to buy the groceries, someone still has to pay the bills. You confront your changed identity every time you do something that used to be done by the person who died. This can be very hard work and, at times, can leave you feeling very drained of emotional, physical, and spiritual energy.

You may occasionally feel childlike as you struggle with your changing identity. You may feel a temporarily heightened dependence on others as well as helplessness, frustration, inadequacy, and fear. These feelings can be overwhelming and scary, but they are actually a natural response to this important need of mourning.

Remember – do what you need to do to survive as you try to re-anchor yourself. To be dependent on others as you struggle with a changing identity does not make you needy or inferior. Your self-identity has been assaulted. Be compassionate with yourself. Reach out for and accept the support of others.

Many people learn that as they work on this need, they ultimately discover some positive aspects of their changed self-identity. For example, you may develop a renewed confidence in yourself. You might reveal a more caring, kind, and sensitive part of yourself. You may develop an assertive part of your identity that empowers you to go on living even though you continue to feel a sense of loss.

Signals That Suggest Potential Inhibition of This Need

In my experience, the primary signals that invite more attention to this need include – but are not limited to – the following: extended shock, searching and yearning, anxiety, explosive emotions, guilt, regret, sadness, and depression.

If you were fortunate enough to have a close day-to-day relationship with the person who died, it is not unusual to experience aspects of extended shock. After all, your own existence feels so very different without them physically here. Your mornings are different, as well as your afternoons, evenings, and nights. The places you go, the activities you do, the conversations you have, the tasks you accomplish — have all changed dramatically. As you experience the shock that they are no longer physically available to you, it can help to devote some dosed time and energy to your changed self-identity. That is, in part, how your signals of shock and numbness eventually soften.

In my experience, searching and yearning, particularly in extremely close relationships, is also quite normal. You might expect the person who died to walk through the door, or think you hear the garage door coming up upon their return home. Yearning is sometimes experienced as, "I can't stop thinking about her," or "All I want to do is be with him again." Reconstructing your self-identity doesn't happen quickly or easily, but some focused work on this need will usually help your signals of searching and yearning soften over time.

What about anxiety? Well, death makes most of us security-craving, routine-lovers feel ill at ease. The person who has died has been a "mirror" to you and now you may naturally feel anxious without them physically here. Your unique relationship with them instinctually impacts your self-identity and sense of security. As C.S. Lewis noted after his wife died, "No one ever told me grief felt so much like fear."

Feeling stuck in guilt and regret might also be a part of your experience when this need is inhibited. There may be aspects of your former self-identity that you struggle with after the death of someone in your life. For example, you could feel you were not as kind to them as you should have been, or you missed important events in their life. Developing a new self-identity includes coming to terms with the reality of one's former self-identity and the limits of your self-responsibility. Exploring any "if onlys…" you might have around your former identity can help you construct your new identity and allow yourself to authentically mourn.

Explosive emotions may also arise, as most of us do not like having our self-identities taken away from us. Protest is often anchored in wishing you could have back what you lost that you valued. With the death of someone who helped you know who you were, your identity has been shattered. You may be upset about both the loss of your old identity and the reality that you are now forced to create a new one.

You might also find that your sadness —feeling pressed down—is symptomatic of a lack of ongoing or effective dosing of this need of mourning. When your life has been intertwined with the person who died, you may feel profound sadness when you realize you eventually must go forward without them. Giving attention to your sadness is a vital part of what can help you work on your changed self-identity.

Questions to Ask Yourself:

These questions are intended to help you see where you are in "dosing" this need. Overall, how do you see yourself doing on developing a new self-identity?

What experiences and activities have you engaged in since the death that have helped you develop a new self-identity?

In what ways did your relationship with the person who died contribute to your self-identity before the death?

What identity changes have you experienced as a result of the death?

What are some things that are challenging for you about the need to develop a new self-identity?

How do you see people treating you differently as a result of your changing identity?

What, if any, positive changes in your self-identity have you noticed since the death?

Active Engagement With Mourning Need 4:

You may have discovered you would benefit from more active dosing of this need. If so, review the below activities and note which ones may be helpful to you as you create your GRIEF PLAN.

1. CREATE A SELF-IDENTITY JOURNAL

If you like to write out your thoughts and feelings, journaling can be an excellent avenue to monitor your changing self-identity. Your inner experiences as you reflect on your identity must be expressed outwardly – and the journal can help you monitor the changes you observe in yourself. In your journal, ask yourself things like: What identity changes have I seen in myself since the death? Are some people treating me differently? If so, how? What, if any, positive changes have I seen in my self-identity? Consider writing out your thoughts about these questions at a consistent time each day so it feels like part of your routine. So that your mind is clear from other distractions, I would recommend each night before you go to bed or first thing when you wake up in the morning.

2. LIMIT ANY BIG CHANGES OR CONCURRENT STRESSES IN YOUR LIFE

As you are faced with the challenge of discovering who you are without the person in your life who died, attempt to keep other stresses or any major life changes to a minimum. Your energy is already likely diminished; don't deplete it even more by making lots of changes or taking on too many tasks. While it may not be entirely possible, try to stay in neutral before you go into gear with additional life changes. Giving yourself permission to slow down as much as possible will help you have better discernment about any changes you may make in the future.

This activity can be done on a big piece of paper or a whiteboard – wherever you have the space to spread out your ideas. In the middle of the space, draw yourself. It doesn't have to be pretty; a stick figure will do just fine. Now, around your figure, write in all the concurrent stresses you have going on in your life. Include things like child and pet care, home maintenance or repairs, work obligations, financial stresses, social obligations, and anything else causing you stress. Include anything related to the death that is on your plate too – perhaps filing required paperwork such as insurance claims or changing car titles. Also include any big changes that may be on the horizon for you – job changes, moves, etc.

Once you have everything down, look at the list as a whole. What can you do to start eliminating stresses? Cross off anything that isn't actually that important. What can be put off? Cross off anything that isn't urgent or doesn't require your attention right now. What items can you delegate to someone else or ask for help with? Write the person's name by the stressor. For the items that are left – the ones that are important, urgent, and can't be delegated – put a star next to them. These are the things to focus on right now as you allow yourself to work on developing your new self-identity without the person who died.

3. CREATE A SANCTUARY JUST FOR YOU

Invite yourself to slow down and go into neutral by creating a safe place for yourself – a private sanctuary where you can go when exploring your new self-identity. Consider furnishing this space with a comfy chair, reading materials, your self-identity journal, and perhaps a way to listen to gentle music. An outside "room" can be equally effective. Do you have a garden, porch, or patio where you can just be? Locate a comfortable chair and consider installing a tabletop fountain to gently flow in the background. For a few minutes each day, retreat into your private sanctuary. Allow the serenity and peace of the space to embrace you as you work on your changing self-identity.

4. REFLECT ON YOUR SELF-ESTEEM

It is normal if your self-esteem was heavily influenced by the person who died. They were likely your mirror – reflecting back to you who you were. Perhaps they were your biggest cheerleader. Or maybe they were the person who would always give you the most honest feedback. They might have been the person you could always turn to when you needed to be nurtured and listened to. Whatever role they played in your life, their absence will often influence your self-esteem as well as your identity.

If you find yourself struggling with your self-esteem since the death, it can be helpful to force yourself to focus on the positive attributes you put out into the world. Set a repeating alarm to go off on your phone every day at the same designated time. When the alarm goes off, stand in front of the nearest mirror. Set a timer and give yourself compliments for three minutes. The compliments can be around anything but try to focus on your character, personality, and talents. While complimenting oneself may not feel natural (and you may need the alarm to force yourself to do it each day), it can help re-frame your self-talk to be more positive. As you go about your day you might find yourself noticing positive attributes to mention next time you go to your mirror.

5. ASSESS ROLE CHANGES THAT ARE THE MOST CHALLENGING FOR YOU

Give attention to the practical role changes that might be naturally difficult for you. For example, if the person who died always managed the finances in your household. Or maybe they were the cook in the family. Or maybe they were the primary driver and you've never had to put gas in your own car before. What is it like for you to take on these new responsibilities while also grieving?

Inventory any new challenges and reflect on how they impact your self-identity. The best thing that you can do for these new challenges is to seek out help. Do you have a friend who can help you learn to balance your checkbook? Can you find a cookbook at the library or online that consists of simple meals? Would it be helpful to take a cooking class with a friend? Can you go to the gas station and ask the attendant for assistance? In many cases, people want to help you – especially after you have experienced the death of someone in your life. Give those around you the opportunity to help you learn to take on these new challenges and build your new self-identity.

6. REFLECT ON ANYONE THAT MAY BE OVER-FUNCTIONING FOR YOU

Sometimes well-meaning family and friends go beyond helping and try to over-function for you. They may be making decisions without even consulting you. For example, if you have an adult child who totally takes over your finances, or they tell you to move in with them because it will "be easier." While they may be well-intentioned, they could, in effect, inhibit your ability to mourn and find your own path out of the dark and into the light.

It is important to set boundaries with anyone who may be over-functioning for you. Sit down with them and tell them that although you appreciate their help, you must make your own way forward. Try to be as clear as you can in outlining what is helpful to you and what is not. Ask them to respect your boundaries and your learning process.

GRIEF PLAN for Need 4:

Write down below the activities you think you can make use of as part of your GRIEF PLAN. Also write out any additional ideas you have that you think might help you dose this need of mourning.

____

____

____

Mourning Need 5: Search for Meaning

"Working on my grief could be considered soul work. Death causes me to become more intimate with myself, others, and the world around me. This journey is an education of my soul, and is manifested in the unfolding of new ways of seeing the world around me."

- The Journey Through Grief

MOURNING NEED 5:
Search for meaning

This need of mourning reminds us that we form bonded relationships with other people to add meaning to our lives.

When someone you love dies, it's normal to question the meaning and purpose of life. You will probably reconsider your life philosophy and explore religious and spiritual values as you work on this need. You may discover yourself searching for meaning in your continued living as you ask "why?" and "how?" questions. "Why did this happen now and in this way?" "How will I be able to go on living my life?" The death reminds you of your lack of control. It can leave you feeling powerless.

The person who died was a part of you. This death means you mourn a loss not only outside of yourself but inside as well. At times, overwhelming sadness and loneliness may be your constant companions. You may feel that when this person died, a part of you died, too. And now you are faced with finding some meaning in going on with your life even though you may at times feel empty.

This death calls for you to consider your spirituality. You may doubt your faith and have spiritual conflicts and questions racing through your head and heart. This is normal and part of your journey toward renewed living.

You might feel distant from your God or higher power, even questioning their existence. You may rage at your God. Such feelings of doubt are normal. Remember – mourners often find themselves questioning their faith for some time before they rediscover meaning in life. But be assured: it can be done, even when you don't have all the answers.

I would be remiss if I didn't warn you to be alert to people who project that if you "have faith," you can bypass the need to mourn. If you internalize this misconception, you will set yourself up to grieve internally but not mourn externally. Having faith does not mean you do not need to mourn. Having faith does mean having the courage to allow yourself to mourn!

It is also important to allow yourself to openly mourn without pressuring yourself to quickly have answers to such profound meaning-of-life questions. Move at your own pace as you recognize that allowing yourself to hurt and finding meaning are not mutually exclusive. Oftentimes, your need to mourn and find meaning in your continued living will blend into each other, with the former giving way to the latter as your grief work continues.

Signals That Suggest Potential Inhibition of This Need

In my experience, the primary signals that invite more attention to this need include – but are not limited to – the following: disorganization, anxiety, explosive emotions, regret, sadness, depression, and difficulties with trust and intimacy.

Allow me to remind you that early in grief it is not unusual to struggle with all of these signals. However, if you feel the signals have become stuck, fixed, or stalled, you can set your intent to give more focused attention to this need of mourning.

A discovery from my counseling experience is that if you don't slowly, over time give attention to this need you will continue to struggle with short-term memory and knowing what to focus on each day. You may move from task to task but not have a sense of accomplishment. In other words, your brain fog will persist. This can reflect that you are naturally struggling with finding a renewed sense of meaning and purpose in your life.

After all, if you have not had the opportunity to recreate a sense of meaning in your life, it is difficult to have a positive attitude related to your future. Meaning and purpose are what motivate us as humans, and a lack of purpose – which is a common consequence when someone we love dies – can leave you feeling lost and alone. Before you can reestablish the "hows" of daily living, you will probably need to give some time and energy to exploring the "whys" of daily living.

I often find that anxiety also relates to this search for meaning need. Loss has invited you into liminal space – "the place betwixt and between." When you are in liminal space, you instinctively feel anxious. It is not only uncomfortable, it is unsettling and frightening.

Anger and explosive emotions may also indicate an inhibition of this mourning need. When your life is "torn apart" it is natural to protest in ways that suggest you don't like your new reality. You may feel a sense of unfairness or injustice about how this death could have happened. This is a meaning-of-life response that is understandable and human. Searching for meaning when you feel things are unfair is never easy. But if you feel stuck with anger and other explosive emotions, this can suggest you would probably benefit from giving more attention to this critical need of mourning.

Regrets and the search for meaning also often go hand-in-hand. This is because the reconstruction of meaning is required as you work to integrate any feelings of regret, guilt, or unfinished business.

Sometimes it means exploring ways to forgive yourself that allow for a new outlook on your life and living. Feeling stuck demands the need to encounter any regret or guilt so you can reconcile them into your continued living. If you carry regret or guilt but don't acknowledge them, you run the risk of losing your divine spark.

Challenges with this need can also be reflected if you feel stuck in sadness and despair. When we as humans are depressed, we can feel like life has no meaning or purpose. Working to understand any feelings of sadness and depression and befriending these signals can help soften them over time. But if you are depressed and deny that to yourself and those around you, the result is often that you stay depressed.

There is often a critical interface between acknowledging the reality of the death and searching for continued meaning in your life. Ask yourself: Have I authentically acknowledged the death, not only with my head but with my heart? If not, don't shame yourself because this is such a central part of the work of mourning.

Do you think that the passage of time is playing a part in where you are with this need? Do you sometimes push parts of the reality away? Revisit the activities from Mourning Need 1 to help dose yourself in acknowledging the reality of the death. Repeat any activities that you found helpful or try something new. While doing the activity, focus on how fully acknowledging the reality of the death allows you to search for continued meaning in your life.

This search for meaning need is naturally slow. Therefore, it can be helpful to remind yourself – "No rewards for speed." However, time spent exploring the questions that follow and engaging in the suggested activities can help soften these care-eliciting signals of your grief.

Questions to Ask Yourself:

These questions are intended to help you see where you are in "dosing" this need. Overall, how do you see yourself doing on searching for meaning?

What experiences and activities have you engaged in since the death that have helped you in your search for meaning?

Do you have any "why?" or "how?" questions right now? If so, what are they?

How have religious, spiritual, or philosophical beliefs played a role in your search for meaning?

In what ways has your understanding of what gives meaning to life changed since the death?

In what ways have you been struggling with finding meaning since the death?

Are there some specific ways you have found continued meaning in your life since the death? If so, what are they?

____

____

____

____

____

____

Active Engagement With Mourning Need 5:

You may have discovered you would benefit from more active dosing of this need. If so, review the below activities and note which ones may be helpful to you as you create your GRIEF PLAN.

1. ALLOW YOURSELF TO QUESTION

When someone we love dies, we naturally question the meaning and purpose of life. Why did this person die? Why are we here? These "why" questions instinctively precede "how" questions. "Why did this happen?" comes before "How will I go on living?" This activity is an invitation to question your philosophy of life and to express your spiritual and/or religious values.

Write down a list of any "why?" questions that have surfaced for you since the death. Find a friend or spiritual counselor who will explore these questions with you without thinking they have to give you answers. As you explore your "why?" questions, be especially patient with yourself. Grief will not heed anyone's timetable – even your own. Say to yourself and aloud, "I'm doing the best that I can as I do my work of mourning. Questioning can be an important part of that."

2. SPEND TIME IN "THIN PLACES"

In the Celtic tradition, "thin places" are spots where the separation between the physical world and the spiritual world seem tenuous. They are places where the veil between heaven and earth, between the holy and the everyday, is so thin that when we are near them, we intuitively sense the timeless, boundless spiritual world. There is a Celtic saying that heaven and earth are only three feet apart, but in thin places that distance is even smaller.

Thin places are usually outdoors, often where water and land meet or land and sky come together. You might find thin places on a riverbank, a beach, or a mountaintop. Being in the great outdoors encourages you to discover what is essential both within you and the world around you. A close relationship with nature grounds your psyche and soul in the spiritual certainty of your roots.

As part of your search for continued meaning in your life, I encourage you to go to a thin place to sit in the sanctuary of stillness. Sitting in stillness with your grief will help you honor the deep voices of quiet wisdom that come forth from within you. As Rainer Maria Rilke observed, "Everything is gestation and then bringing forth." Sitting in stillness helps restore your divine spark.

The integration of grief and discovering renewed meaning in your life after loss is born out of stillness, not frantic movement forward. When you overcome any instinct to attempt to "manage" your grief, other impulses such as grace, wisdom, love, and truth come forth. It is through sitting in stillness that your soul is ever so slowly restored. Sit in your thin place and recognize that the rhythm of stillness is the teacher of contentment and peace.

3. START EACH DAY WITH A MEDITATION OR PRAYER

For many mourners, waking up in the morning is one of the hardest parts of their day. It's as if each time you awaken, you must confront anew the realization that someone you love is gone. Starting the day off with tears and a heavy heart, day in and day out, is so draining. Yet it may be a necessary, unavoidable part of your grief journey.

However, it may help to start each day by setting the tone with praying or meditating first thing in the morning. When you wake up, stretch before getting out of bed or picking up your phone. Feel the blood coursing through your body. Listen to the hum of your consciousness. Repeat a simple affirmation or prayer to yourself, such as: "Today I will honor my grief. Today I will appreciate my life." You might also offer words of gratitude: "Thank you for giving me this day. Help me to appreciate it, be present to it, and make it count."

4. GO TO EXILE

Choosing to spend time alone is an essential self-nurturing spiritual practice as you search for renewed meaning in your life. It affords the opportunity to be unaffected by others' wants and needs.

It is impossible to really know yourself if you never take time to withdraw from the demands of daily living. Alone time does not mean you are being selfish. Instead, you will experience rest and renewal in ways you otherwise would not. A lack of alone time often results in heightened confusion and a muting of your life force. Your human spirit is naturally compassionate, and once you feel restored, your instinct to find continued meaning in your life will be renewed.

Within your exiled time and space will come insights that rise to the surface only in stillness and with dedicated time to authentically mourn. So, while mourning requires you not over-isolate, scheduling alone time on a regular basis can be restorative. Don't shut out your family and friends altogether, but do answer the call for contemplative solitude. Go to your calendar and put aside dedicated solitude time this week.

5. ORGANIZE A TREE PLANTING

Trees represent the beauty, vibrancy, and continuity of life. A specially selected, located, and planted tree can honor the person who died and serve as a perennial memorial. You might plan a short ceremony for the tree planting. You might also consider a personalized marker or sign.

For a more private option, plant a tree in your own yard. Consult your local nursery for an appropriate selection. Flowering trees are especially beautiful in the spring. You might also consider a variety of tree that the person who died loved or that reminds you of a place that was special to them.

6. NAME YOUR GRATITUDE

When someone has died that brought meaning to your life, it can be difficult to feel a sense of gratitude. After all, you have been "torn apart." Yet, gratitude prepares you for the things that eventually bring meaning and purpose back into your life. Reflect for a moment – somehow you have survived. Looking back you may recognize the many supporting gestures, big and small, you have been offered along this grief journey. When you fill your life with gratitude you invoke a self-fulfilling prophecy. What you expect to happen can happen. For example, if you don't expect anyone to support you in your grief, they often don't. By contrast, if you anticipate support and nurturance, you will likely find it.

This activity invites and encourages you to think of all you have to be thankful for. Doing so does not in any way deny your sense of loss and the need to mourn. You are allowing yourself to be self-compassionate when you reflect on the things that make your life worth living. Give conscious thought to the possibilities for continued meaning in your life. Honor those possibilities and have gratitude for them.

Be grateful if you have good health. Be grateful for your family and friends who have been able and willing to support you during this difficult time in your life. Above all, be grateful for this very moment. When you are grateful you are actively dosing your search for meaning need. When you feel ready start a gratitude journal. At first you may find this challenging, but as you make this a daily practice, it will get easier and more joyful.

GRIEF PLAN for Need 5:

Write down below the activities you think you can make use of as part of your GRIEF PLAN. Also write out any additional ideas you have that you think might help you dose this need of mourning.

Mourning Need 6: Let Others Help You – Now and Always

"I heal, in part, by allowing others to express their love for me. By choosing to invite others into my journey, I move toward health and healing."

– The Journey Through Grief

MOURNING NEED 6:
Let others help you— now and always

This need of mourning is about allowing yourself to seek and accept support. The quality and quantity of understanding support you get during your work of mourning will have a major influence on your capacity to integrate this loss into your life. You cannot – nor should you try to – do this alone. Drawing on the experiences and encouragement of friends, fellow grievers, and grief-informed counselors is not a weakness but a healthy human need. And because mourning naturally unfolds over time, this support must be available long after the death of someone in your life.

As previously noted, because our society places so much value on the ability to "carry on," "keep your chin up," and "keep busy," many grieving people are abandoned shortly after the event of the death. "It's best not to talk about it," "It's over and done with," and "It's time to get on with your life" are the types of messages directed at grieving people that all too often dominate. Obviously, this thinking encourages you to deny or repress your grief rather than embrace and express it.

If you know people who consider themselves supportive yet offer you these kinds of mourning avoidant attitudes, you will need to look to others for truly helpful support. People who see your mourning as something that should be overcome or gone around instead of experienced will not help you come out of the dark and into the light.

To be truly helpful, the people in your support system must appreciate the impact this death has had on you. They must understand that in order to heal, you must be allowed – even encouraged – to mourn long after the death. Again, they must encourage you to see mourning not as an enemy to be vanquished but rather as a necessity to be experienced as a result of having loved.

Signals That Suggest Potential Inhibition of This Need

In my experience, the primary signals that invite more attention to this need include – but are not limited to – the following: disbelief, anxiety, sadness, depression, and difficulties with trust and intimacy.

A prolonged sense of disbelief and numbness sometimes reflects a challenge with this need of mourning. If you have lacked support or found yourself rejecting support since the death, it naturally puts you at risk for grieving internally but not having a social context that invites and encourages you to mourn outwardly. Lack of support makes it more difficult to re-story your life in ways that help you dose the linchpin need of mourning – acknowledge the reality of the death. As a result, your psychic numbing continues to try to get your attention. When support is lacking or not accepted, you are at risk for staying in a perpetual state of disbelief. You may feel like you are living in a bubble, insulated from the truth of what happened.

Anxiety is another emotion I have observed when there is an inhibition around receiving and accepting ongoing support from others. You need and deserve support as you explore instinctive questions that often result after a death. Questions like, "How will I survive and go on without the person who died?" and "Who or what could possibly fill the void I'm feeling?" If you have tried to ask yourself questions about your fears without the support of people around you, the natural result is often unease and anxiety.

Intractable sadness and depression can also suggest a lack of grief support. As I have noted as a theme in this book, grief must be converted into active mourning. If your sadness and depression seem to persist you may want to ask yourself: Have I been openly and authentically dosing my need to mourn?

Similarly, difficulties with trust and intimacy are often clues to an inhibition of this need. I often say that if you don't mourn well it is hard to love well. Finding people who provide the safety you need to mourn is essential to your ultimate well-being. All of these above signals only soften if you give yourself permission to openly and honestly mourn. And, as a reminder, mourning requires seeking and accepting support.

Questions to Ask Yourself:

These questions are intended to help you see where you are in "dosing" this need. Overall, how do you see yourself doing on seeking and accepting support?

What experiences and activities have you engaged in since the death that you let others help you – now and always?

Do you feel that people around you are able to support you in your grief?

Which people or groups in your life have been good supporters since the death?

Which people in your life have been largely absent since the death?

Are there any circumstances around the death that you believe have made it more difficult to seek and accept support?

Has anyone been toxic in their interactions with you since the death? What, if anything, are you doing to set boundaries with these people?

How would you rate yourself on your ability to seek and accept support from other people? Please explain:

Has the support you accessed changed any as time has progressed since the death? If so, how:

Active Engagement With Mourning Need 6:

You may have discovered you would benefit from more active dosing of this need. If so, review the below activities and note which ones may be helpful to you as you create your GRIEF PLAN.

1. RECOGNIZE THAT YOUR FRIENDSHIPS WILL PROBABLY CHANGE

Mourners often tell me how surprised and hurt they feel when friends fall away after a death. "I found out who my friends really are," they say. Know that just as you are doing the best you can right now, your friends are doing the best they can, too—even if it doesn't seem that way. Unfortunately, grief makes some people feel very awkward and uncomfortable. This naturally affects their ability to be of support to you.

The best way for you to respond in the face of faltering friendships is to be proactive and honest. Even though you are the one who is grieving, you may need to be the one to phone your friends and keep in touch. When you do talk to them, be honest. Tell them how you are truly feeling and that you need and appreciate their support. If you find that certain friends can't handle your grief talk, try sticking to lighter topics with them and lean more heavily on the friends who can be present to whatever you are experiencing.

Over time, you will probably notice a natural attrition among your friends. Some may fade away and never come back. You will need to mourn these losses, though you will likely also find that other friendships deepen and new ones emerge.

By contrast, maybe you are one of the fortunate people who feel tremendous support and love from your family and friends. If so, rejoice that you have such wise and wonderful companions in your life, and when opportunities arise, offer them the same empathy and presence in return.

As you inventory your changing friendships, it may be helpful to keep a list of those around you. As you learn in what ways they can and can't support you, you can make notes on the list by their names. This can be helpful when you need someone to reach out to for discussion of a deeper, heavy topic, or to find someone to reach out to for lighter fare. Whatever support you need right now – hopefully you'll be able to find it on your list.

2. REACH OUT AND TOUCH

For many people, physical contact with another human being is comforting. In fact, it's one of Gary Chapman's five love languages. That's because touch has bodily effects. When we are touched in comforting ways, our brains are flooded with dopamine, serotonin, and oxytocin.

These feel-good hormones help regulate our mood and make us feel calmer and happier. What's more, touch stimulates the vagus nerve, which branches out throughout our entire bodies. Its role is to calm the nervous system, which in turn helps boost our immune system and can lower our blood pressure and heart rate.

Have you hugged anyone lately? Held someone's hand? Put your arm around another human being? Hug someone you feel safe with. Kiss your children or a friend's baby. Walk arm in arm with a neighbor. If you are soothed by touch, you might also appreciate massage, reiki, or another type of touch therapy. Try a session and see how it feels for you.

3. FIND A GRIEF "BUDDY"

While no one else will grieve this death just like you, there are often many people who have had similar experiences. We are rarely totally alone in our grief. I encourage you to seek out and locate a grief "buddy" – someone who is also in mourning, someone you can talk to, someone who also needs a companion in grief right now. You might ask a grieving friend, neighbor, or colleague to join you, or you might find a grief buddy at a grief support group. Make a pact with your grief buddy to call each other whenever one of you needs to talk. Promise to listen without judgment. Commit to spending time together. You might arrange to meet once a week for breakfast or lunch with your grief buddy.

4. IGNORE HURTFUL ADVICE

Sometimes well-meaning family and friends will hurt you unknowingly with their words or actions. For example, you may be told:

- "I know exactly how you feel"
- "It is time to get on with your life"
- "Keep your chin up and keep busy"
- "This is a blessing in disguise"

- "You can still have other children"
- "Now you have an angel in Heaven"
- "Time heals all wounds"
- "God wouldn't give you anything more than you can bear"
- "Just be strong and put it behind you"

While it may be challenging, allow yourself to have grace and try not to take these kinds of comments to heart. These "thought-stopping clichés" are often offered up because people don't know what else to say. The problem is: phrases like these diminish your unique and significant loss. When you feel up to it, you can provide some supportive education when someone tries to comfort you with clichés. Say: "I'm sure you are trying to be helpful, but would it be okay if I share with you why I don't find your words supportive?" Then, if they accept your invitation, you can go on to teach them what you do find to be helpful.

5. ALLOW YOURSELF TO RECEIVE

Many of us are better at giving than receiving. Yet, there is a reciprocal relationship between these two. In order to receive, we must give. And in order to give, we must receive.

I encourage you to give the following a try. Select a supportive friend or your "grief buddy" to assist you with the following: Sit across from your friend. Be silent for two to three minutes, then have your friend tell you something they admire or appreciate about you.

Take in what your friend shares with you with an open heart. Notice when you are uncomfortable or find yourself wanting to discount what your friend says. Breathe deeply for a minute as you continue to open yourself to this gift of receiving. Sit with it until you can fully accept the verbal gift. Show your gratitude by saying "thank you" aloud. Observe how your connection and bond with your friend deepens. As you allow yourself to receive, any separation between you and your friend disappears. Congratulate yourself for being able to receive!

6. DEDICATE SOMETHING

After a death, one long-cherished convention is to dedicate something in memory of the person. The thing that is dedicated might range from a park bench or newly planted tree to a set of library books, a scholarship, a charitable donation, a performance, or a building. You can choose to dedicate anything you'd like and turn it into an opportunity to seek out and accept support from other grievers.

Gather a group of people who also knew and loved the person who died, perhaps on their birthday, the anniversary of their death, or another important day to them. It could be just close friends and family, or a much larger public group. Make it as much of an event as you can – play music, offer refreshments, and consider having a large photo. As you explain to the group why you have decided to dedicate this item in honor of the person who died, share with them your memories of the person. Tell them that you'd also like to hear their memories. As you mingle with the other attendees, consider all the people who loved and were impacted by the person who died. Dedicating something in honor of the person who died helps you connect with people. Making these connections can result in strengthening the bonds of love that make life seem worth living again.

GRIEF PLAN for Need 6:

Write down below the activities you think you can make use of as part of your GRIEF PLAN. Also write out any additional ideas you have that you think might help you dose this need of mourning.

SUMMARY OF YOUR GRIEF PLAN

Review all the notes you made following each need of mourning that will help you put your GRIEF PLAN into action. Transfer the most important points from each need to the spaces provided on the next two pages.

Working Your GRIEF PLAN: Dosing the Six Needs of Mourning

Thank you for letting me outline these six needs of mourning and help you make a plan to put your grief into action. What an honor to companion you during one of the most challenging journeys of your life. Upholding and dosing these six needs can and will help you understand how you have been transformed by this loss. My experience with thousands of people in grief is that the consequences of not attending to these six needs can result in being among what I refer to as the "living dead." I don't want you to be stuck in your grief and lose your divine spark. Remember – actively engaging with these essential needs will help you eventually go on to live fully until you die.

NEED	ACTIVITIES
MOURNING NEED 1: Acknowledge the reality of the death	
MOURNING NEED 2: Embrace the pain of the loss	
MOURNING NEED 3: Remember the person who died	
MOURNING NEED 4: Develop a new self-identity	
MOURNING NEED 5: Search for meaning	
MOURNING NEED 6: Let others help you—now and always	

OTHER IDEAS

RECONCILING YOUR GRIEF

Reconciliation is the term I find most appropriate for the healing that evolves as you work your GRIEF PLAN. It originates from Middle English and means "to make your life good again." No, we as humans don't get over grief. We don't forget our losses. Instead, if we mourn them well, our losses become part of who we are.

I'm sometimes asked, "How do I know when I'm experiencing reconciliation?" You will know that you are moving toward reconciliation when you start to feel lighter. Your thoughts and feelings will begin to seem softer and gentler. You will begin to feel more energetic and hopeful.

With reconciliation comes full acknowledgment of the reality of the death. Beyond a cognitive working through of the death, there's also an emotional and spiritual accommodation. What has been understood at the head level is now understood at the heart level. Confidence is renewed and the desire to become reinvolved with the activities of living is reawakened. There is also often a deepening wisdom about the fact that pain and grief are difficult, yet necessary, parts of life.

Your Patchwork Heart

Your heart has been broken, maybe even torn into a million pieces by the death of someone you love. Active, intentional mourning is the process of stitching it back together.

As you approach reconciliation, your heart will become whole again. But it will be a patchwork heart. The seams where it has been sewn together will always be apparent to you, and they will twinge and ache sometimes. The wounds will be healed, yet the scars will always remain. The good news is that as you work your GRIEF PLAN you will be able to live wholeheartedly again, because your torn-apart heart will be mended.

Signs of Reconciliation

To help you discern where you are in your movement toward reconciliation at any given time, the following list of signs of integrating this loss into your life may be helpful. This list may give you a way to monitor your movement through grief. As new reconciliation signs arise while you work your GRIEF PLAN, you may find it helpful to place checkmarks next to them. The more you actively allow yourself to engage in the six needs of mourning, the more signs you will probably notice. Place a checkmark beside the signs you feel you have experienced at this point in time.

- ☐ You can acknowledge the reality and finality of the death
- ☐ You can return to stable eating and sleeping patterns
- ☐ You are no longer consistently exhausted
- ☐ You can find something to laugh about and enjoy your hobbies again
- ☐ You can experience meaningful friendships and relationships
- ☐ You can feel a sense of self-worth and self-respect
- ☐ You can organize and plan your life toward the future while continuing to remember the past
- ☐ You can have the serenity to be comfortable with the way things are rather than attempting to make things as they were
- ☐ You can realize unhelpful comments made by others are made in ignorance
- ☐ You can have the versatility to welcome more change into your life

- [ ] You can understand that you do not "get over" or have complete "closure" of your grief
- [ ] You can become acquainted with new parts of yourself that you have discovered in your grief journey
- [ ] You can acknowledge that the pain of grief is a consequence of having the capacity to give and receive love
- [ ] You can reach out to help someone else when you see they are in need of support
- [ ] You can have a sense of renewed meaning and purpose in your life

Usually there is not one great moment of "arrival" of reconciliation, but instead a series of subtle changes and incremental progress. Along the way, I hope you will stop and take the time to notice and be grateful for even very small advancements. If you're beginning to taste your food again, be thankful. If you mustered the energy to meet a friend for lunch, be grateful. If you finally got a good night's sleep, rejoice.

As you work your GRIEF PLAN, I urge you to remember to be patient and gentle with yourself along the way. There is no deadline. There is not always forward motion. Sometimes it may feel like you are going backwards. But as you actively dose the six needs of mourning and utilize the activities you have selected for your GRIEF PLAN, the sooner you are likely to find yourself soothed by the balm of reconciliation. Yes, reconciled grief results in transformation – "an entire change in form." Yet, ultimately many of us grievers discover courageous, honorable, and joyful parts of ourselves. Work your GRIEF PLAN as an active intentional process and you will come out of the dark and into the light!

A FINAL WORD

Thank you for allowing me the privilege of helping you create your GRIEF PLAN. My sincere hope is that as you work your plan, it will help you understand, embrace, and express your grief. When all is said and done, you love, you come to grief, and you have six needs to dose as you allow yourself to authentically mourn. May you continue to discover the freedom to live life with a renewed divine spark.

If you picked up this book, it is probably because you realize your grief is trying to get your attention. You have now committed yourself to giving your grief the time and expression it needs and deserves. Give yourself permission to take as much time as you need for your signals to soften and for you to feel like you are reaching a place of reconciliation. Do remember – there are no rewards for speed in grief. I encourage you to find the pace and the activities that work for you.

No, you did not ask for this loss. But it has come to you, and you have learned the importance of allowing yourself to mourn openly and honestly. You have learned to authentically mourn. If you give up, your spirit dies. I hope you never give up and that you choose to mourn well, so you can live well and love well.

May you keep your heart open wide and receptive to what life brings you, both happy and sad. And, in doing so, may you create a pathway to living your life with meaning and purpose each and every day.

I hope we meet one day!

ABOUT THE AUTHOR

Alan D. Wolfelt, Ph.D. is a respected author and educator on the topics of companioning others and healing in grief. He serves as Director of the Center for Loss and Life Transition and is on the faculty at the University of Colorado Medical School's Department of Family Medicine. Dr. Wolfelt has written many bestselling books on healing in grief, including *Understanding Your Grief, Grief One Day at a Time*, and *First Aid for Broken Hearts.* Visit www. centerforloss.com to learn more about grief and loss and to order Dr. Wolfelt's books.

ALSO BY ALAN WOLFELT

Understanding Your Grief

Since its debut in 1992, this favorite by one of the world's most beloved grief counselors has found a place in the homes and hearts of hundreds of thousands of mourners across the globe. Filled with compassion and hope, *Understanding Your Grief* helps you understand and befriend your painful, complex, yet normal thoughts and feelings after the death of someone loved. *Understanding Your Grief* is built on Dr. Wolfelt's Ten Touchstones—basic principles to learn and actions to take to help yourself engage with your grief and create momentum toward healing. This second edition includes concise additional wisdom on new topics such as the myth of closure, complicated and traumatic grief, grief overload, loneliness, the power of ritual, and more. Excellent as an empathetic handbook for anyone in mourning as well as a text for support groups, *Understanding Your Grief* also pairs with *The Understanding Your Grief Journal.*

If you're grieving a death or a significant loss of any kind, this refreshed bestseller will be your rock and steadfast companion as you journey through the wilderness of your unique grief.

"After almost four years on the grief path, this is by far the best book I've read to date. I wish I had it at the start of my journey. I recommend this book to everyone I know."

ISBN 978-1-61722-307-5 • 215 pages • softcover • $14.95

ALL DR. WOLFELT'S PUBLICATIONS CAN BE ORDERED BY MAIL FROM:

Companion Press | 3735 Broken Bow Road | Fort Collins, CO 80526
(970) 226-6050 | www.centerforloss.com

ALSO BY ALAN WOLFELT

Grief One Day at a Time: 365 Meditations to Help You Heal After Loss

After someone you love dies, each day can be a struggle. But each day, you can also find comfort and understanding in this daily companion. With one brief entry for every day of the calendar year, this little book offers small, one-day-at-a-time doses of guidance and healing. Each entry includes an inspiring or soothing quote followed by a short discussion of the day's theme.

How do you get through the loss of a loved one? One day at a time. This compassionate gem of a book will accompany you.

"Each day I look forward to reading a new page…I can't imagine dealing with my sorrow without [this] book."

ISBN 978-1-61722-238-2 • 384 pages • softcover • $14.95

ALSO BY ALAN WOLFELT

The Journey Through Grief: Reflections on Healing

SECOND EDITION

This revised, second edition of *The Journey Through Grief* takes Dr. Wolfelt's popular book of reflections and adds space for guided journaling, asking readers thoughtful questions about their unique mourning needs and providing room to write responses.

The Journey Through Grief is organized around the six needs that all mourners must yield to—indeed embrace—if they are to go on to find continued meaning in life and living. Following a short explanation of each mourning need is a series of brief, spiritual passages that, when read slowly and reflectively, help mourners work through their unique thoughts and feelings.

"Dr. Wolfelt reminds us that it is not only the physical and emotional but also the spiritual that needs to be explored in our journeys through grief. He breathes hope for healing into our hearts. This book is stirring and abundantly encouraging to all mourners."

ISBN 978-1-87965-111-1 • 144 pages • hardcover • $19.95